Migration and Citizenship

IMISCOE **(International Migration, Integration and Social Cohesion)**

IMISCOE is a European Commission-funded Network of Excellence of more than 350 scientists from various research institutes that specialise in migration and integration issues in Europe. These researchers, who come from all branches of the economic and social sciences, the humanities and law, implement an integrated, multidisciplinary and internationally comparative research programme that focuses on Europe's migration and integration challenges.

Within the programme, existing research is integrated and new research lines are developed that involve issues crucial to European-level policy-making and provide a theory-based design to implement new research.

The publication program of IMISCOE is based on five distinct publication profiles, designed to make its research and results available to scientists, policy makers and the public at large. High quality manuscripts written by IMISCOE members, or in cooperation with IMISCOE members, are published in these five series. An Editorial Committee coordinates the review process of the manuscripts. The five series are:
1. Joint Studies
2. Research
3. Reports
4. Dissertations
5. Training

More information on the network can be found at: www.imiscoe.org

IMISCOE **Reports** include a broader array of documents such as collections of working papers, conference proceedings and annual reports from the IMISCOE network.

Migration and Citizenship

Legal Status, Rights and Political Participation

Rainer Bauböck (editor)

IMISCOE Reports
AMSTERDAM UNIVERSITY PRESS

Cover design: Studio Jan de Boer BNO, Amsterdam
Lay-out: Fito Prepublishing, Almere

ISBN-13   978 90 5356 888 0
ISBN-10   90 5356 888 3
NUR   741 / 763

© Amsterdam University Press, Amsterdam 2006

All rights reserved. Without limiting the rights under copyright reserved above, no part of this book may be reproduced, stored in or introduced into a retrieval system, or transmitted, in any form or by any means (electronic, mechanical, photocopying, recording or otherwise) without the written permission of both the copyright owner and the author of the book.

Contents

Text Boxes 7

Tables 8

Introduction 9
Rainer Bauböck

1 **Citizenship and migration – concepts and controversies** 15
   Rainer Bauböck
   Introduction 15
   Citizenship status 16
   Citizenship rights and duties 23
   Citizenship virtues and practices 31

2 **The legal status of immigrants and their access to nationality** 33
   Albert Kraler
   The legal status of foreign nationals 33
   Citizenship regulations in comparative perspective:
      Is there convergence? 40
   Access to, acquisition of and loss of nationality in liberal states –
      is there convergence or divergence? 44
   Explaining citizenship policies in liberal states 51
   Dual citizenship 58
   Migrant choices, the impact of policies on naturalisation
      behaviour and the consequences of naturalisation 60
   Perspectives for research 65

3 **EU citizenship and the status of third country nationals** 67
   Bernhard Perchinig
   The roots of Union citizenship 67
   Union citizenship or European denizenship? 70
   European citizenship and policies vis-à-vis third country
      nationals 72
   European citizenship and antidiscrimination 79
   The concept of civic citizenship 80

4 **Political participation, mobilisation and representation of immigrants and their offspring in Europe** 83
Marco Martiniello
Introduction 83
Definitions and concepts 84
The thesis of political quiescence of immigrants 85
Explaining the various forms of immigrant political participation 87
A typology of the various forms of immigrant political participation in the country of settlement 90
Transnational political participation 98
Research perspectives 101
How to evaluate political participation of immigrants and their offspring in the country of residence? 102

Annex 106

Notes 113

References 119

Text Boxes

Text Box 1: *Alexander I. Gray, Goizane Mota*, Integration management in the Basque country: citizenship disconnected from nationality 34
Text Box 2: *Gianluca Parolin*, Citizenship and the Arab world 49
Text Box 3: *Tanja Wunderlich*, Migrants' motivations to naturalise 54
Text Box 4: *Dilek Çinar*, The politics of external citizenship – the case of Turkey 58
Text Box 5: *Jean-Louis Rallu*, Naturalisation, a factor of economic integration? 64
Text Box 6: *Anne Walter*, A right to family reunification 77
Text Box 7: *Anja Van Heelsum*, Research on voting behaviour of ethnic groups in the Netherlands 89
Text Box 8: *Davide Però*, The 'comedy' of participation: immigrant consultation in southern European cities 94
Text Box 9: *Anja Van Heelsum*, Research on civic participation in the Netherlands 97
Text Box 10: *Anja Van Heelsum*, Research on the civic community perspective in the Netherlands 104

Tables

Table 1: *Harald Waldrauch*, Acquisition of nationality at birth and by naturalisation in Western Europe (15 old EU Member States, Norway and Switzerland)   106

Table 2: *Harald Waldrauch*, Voting rights of third country nationals in Western Europe (25 EU states, Norway and Switzerland)   110

Introduction

Rainer Bauböck

Citizenship has emerged as an important topic of research on migration and migrant integration since the 1980s. Before this there was little connection between migration research and the legal literature on nationality law or political theories and sociological analyses of citizenship in a broader sense. This mutual disinterest is not difficult to understand. On the one hand, in traditional overseas countries of immigration, immigrants' access to citizenship and eventual naturalisation was taken for granted as a step in a broader process of assimilation. On the other hand, in Europe the largest immigration contingents had emerged from the recruitment of guestworkers who had been invited to stay only temporarily and were never perceived as future citizens.

Both perceptions were eventually undermined when the dynamics of the migration process interacted with political developments towards a more inclusive conception of citizenship. Family reunification turned guestworkers into settled immigrants. Many among these maintained, however, strong ties to their countries of origin. For these migrants, retaining the nationality of origin was a natural choice both for its instrumental value as a bundle of rights and because of its symbolic value as a marker of ethno-national identity. At the same time, the rights of permanent residents in major democratic receiving states were upgraded in many areas or equalised with those of citizens. Finally, more and more countries of immigration abandoned the existing consensus in international law that those who naturalise have to renounce their previous nationality and a growing number of sending countries also accepted multiple nationality among their expatriates. All these developments have blurred the previously clear line separating aliens from citizens. This could not remain without consequences. While some observers welcomed these trends as heralding a new cosmopolitan era in which state-bound citizenship would eventually be overcome, others were concerned about migrants' multiple loyalties, their apparent free-riding on citizenship rights without duties and their political mobilisation according to ethnic or religious identities.

In this report we trace the main steps in these developments, summarise the state of research and emphasise controversies between competing interpretations. The report does not, however, aim at a comprehensive and high level overview. It reflects approaches that have guided past research carried out by members of the IMISCOE cluster on citizenship, legal status and political participation and it points towards a future research agenda to which the cluster hopes to contribute.

The concepts of political opportunity structure, political integration and political transnationalism outline complementary research perspectives on migration and citizenship.

Since the start of the IMISCOE network the cluster has met twice in workshops held in Vienna in July 2004[1] and in Coimbra in December of the same year. Our cluster is composed of members from various disciplines, among them political science, sociology, law, history, anthropology and demography, that all have their own conceptions of citizenship and use a variety of different quantitative and qualitative research methodologies. This heterogeneity poses obvious difficulties in developing a common research agenda, but it also helps to shed light on the blind spots of each discipline by combining different perspectives. In our debates within the cluster we have so far achieved an initial step towards future interdisciplinary research. We have identifed a small number of analytical concepts that provide common reference points in our analyses of migrant citizenship, legal status and political participation. This introduction will shortly discuss three of these concepts and illustrate which research perspectives they open.

The first among these concepts is a society's political opportunity structure. This concept has been widely used in research on migrants' political behaviour and activities, including voter turnout and representation in political bodies, membership in political parties and organisations, lobbying, public claims-making and protest movements. The political opportunity structure consists of laws that allocate different statuses and rights to various groups of migrants and formally constrain or enable their activities, of institutions of government and public administration in which migrants are or are not represented, of public policies that address migrants' claims, concerns and interests or do not, and of a public culture that is inclusive and accepts diversity or that supports national homogeneity and a myth of shared ancestry. When we describe all these elements of a political system as an opportunity structure, we emphasise that migrants are not only objects of laws, policies and discourses but also agents, who pursue their interests either individually or collectively. From this perspective, the point of analysing a political opportunity structure is to identify institutional incentives and disincentives that help to explain migrants' choices of political strategies. This need not imply that these choices are always rational ones or that they generally achieve their goals.

There is, however, an alternative research perspective that regards the political opportunity structure not as given and as explaining migrants' activities but is instead interested in explaining how these structures change over time and in comparing them across countries, regions or cities. This research agenda includes not only institutionalist approaches but also normative political theories, comparative law, political discourse and policy-making analyses. Combining the two perspectives helps to understand feedback loops, i.e. changes in an opportunity structure as a result of political migrants' choices and activities. Such interactions between structure and agency have been at the centre of much contemporary sociological theory. However, making these relevant for empirical research requires bringing together researchers who work predominantly within one of the two perspectives. This is what we hope to achieve in our cluster where researchers focusing on migrants' political participation cooperate with others who compare citizenship policies between European states or cities.

A second core concept in our cluster is political integration. In the IMISCOE network four out of nine research clusters deal with various dimensions of immigrant integration, focusing on political, economic, social and cultural integration respectively. Integration in a broad sense refers to a condition of societal cohesion as well as to a process of inclusion of outsiders or newcomers. In contrast with 'assimilation'[2], integration in the latter sense is generally defined as a two-way process of interaction between given institutions of a society and those who gain access that will also result in changing the institutional framework and the modes of societal cohesion. In this interpretation, integration brings together the two perspectives discussed above with regard to opportunity structures, but it is more normatively loaded in its connotations of societal cohesion. Some researchers have therefore preferred to use alternative terms such as inclusion or incorporation. The main disadvantage of these terms, apart from being less popular outside the academic world, is that they are generally only used transitively. Societies include or incorporate migrants, but these do not include or incorporate themselves.

The concept of integration is open for both transitive and intransitive use. On the one hand, political integration can be regarded as an aspect of structural integration. In this sense it refers to access to political status, rights, opportunities and representation for immigrants and an equalisation of these conditions between native and immigrant populations. On the other hand, political integration is also about migrants' activities and participation, and it refers normatively to their acceptance of the laws, institutional framework and political values that 'integrate' a political system. The normative aspects of integration should always be made explicit and they may sometimes for good reasons be challenged. For our research agenda it is important to reject a nationalist perspective, from which immigrants raise an integration problem whenever they do not fit a preconceived definition of national community. At the same time, we must remain aware that immigrant exclusion and social marginalisation may breed forms of political radicalism and religious fanaticism that create serious threats for democratic polities.

In Europe, the term political integration has yet another meaning that refers to the pooling or transfer of state sovereignty within the European Union. The significance of Union citizenship and the direct impact of European integration on citizenship policies of the Member States is quite limited. However, there is a nascent European citizenship regime that has historically emerged from rights of free movement for nationals of the Member States and is now hesitantly embracing the harmonisation of legal status, rights and integration policies for third country nationals.

Research on migrants' political integration focuses on the post-migration stage in the receiving society. Circular migration patterns, immigrants' links to their countries of origin, and these countries' policies towards their expatriates may be taken into account as external factors but will generally be regarded as obstacles for integration or indicators for an integration deficit. This is a serious limitation of the concept that can be overcome by expanding research towards transnational arenas and activities. Political transnationalism is the third core concept that informs our approach to the migration-citizenship nexus. Studies on migrant transnationalism challenge the separation between the migration and integration stages. Research on political transnationalism has focused mostly on migrants' political identities and activities in relation to their countries of origin. However, the concept applies as well to the status of external citizenship and to sending country policies vis-à-vis emigrant communities and the destination state. Finally, transnational citizenship has also been interpreted as a broader transformation of political membership in migration contexts that is most visibly manifested in the proliferation of multiple nationality. While a transnational research perspective transcends a focus on integration in the receiving society, it can be used to broaden the notion of political opportunity structure so that it includes states of origin as well as transnational migrant networks and diasporic communities dispersed over several countries.

The four chapters of this report discuss general theories and research perspectives on citizenship and migration (chapter 1), comparative analyses of legal status of foreign nationals and acquisition and loss of nationality (chapter 2), the emerging European citizenship regime (chapter 3), and migrants' political participation and representation (chapter 4). Conclusions that are relevant for future research are presented in boxes. Summaries of research on these topics by IMISCOE partners and research teams with whom we cooperate are highlighted in framed text boxes in chapters two, three and four. The annex of the report presents tables with updated information on major rules of access to nationality and on voting rights for third country nationals in EU Member States.

We identify four general tasks for research on migration and citizenship:
a) comparing institutions and policies of citizenship that respond to migration within and across countries;
b) assessing the consistency of these responses with legal norms, their legitimacy in terms of political norms and their consequences and effectiveness in achieving policy goals;
c) studying the impact of migration on changes of institutional arrangements and policies;
d) analysing migrant attitudes, ties and practices with regard to citizenship: their senses of belonging to political communities, their involvement in different polities through social, economic, cultural and political ties, their choices with regard to alternative statuses of citizenship, their use of rights, their compliance with duties and their political activities.

These tasks require cooperation between different academic disciplines, especially, but not exclusively, between law, political science, sociology, history and anthropology. The topic of migration and citizenship is also at the heart of many public debates and public policy making. The IMISCOE network brings together researchers from these disciplines and offers a platform for dialogue between researchers, journalists and policy makers.

1 Citizenship and migration – concepts and controversies

Rainer Bauböck

Introduction

Citizenship is a very old concept that has undergone many transformations. Since the times of Athenian democracy and the Roman Republic its core meaning has been a status of membership in a self-governing political community. This idea has been revived at every transition from authoritarian regimes to democratic ones. However, this is not the only meaning of citizenship. In periods of decline or absence of popular rule, the concept has been often reduced to a formal legal status with certain attached privileges or duties guaranteed or enforced by political authorities. In contemporary liberal democracies political citizenship has to compete with other affiliations in all kinds of associations, organisations, or communities in civil society. Recent governmental discourses about citizenship also tend to emphasise virtues of self-reliance and the responsibilities of individuals to contribute to the wider society more than active participation in political life (Smith 2001).

This report does not aspire to discuss all facets of the history of the concept and contemporary citizenship discourses.[1] It will use citizenship in its broad political meaning that refers to individual membership, rights and participation in a polity and it has a specific thematic focus on conceptions of citizenship and comparative research questions that emerge from migration studies. Studying migrants' social networks and organisations as well as their cultural and religious identities is still crucially important since these are among the most important factors influencing their political opportunities and activities. Our research agenda differs thus from other clusters in the IMISCOE network in its focus on citizenship as the object of study, not in the context variables that we consider when explaining citizenship policies or migrants' choices and political behaviour.

Migration highlights the political core and the boundaries of citizenship.

In migration contexts, citizenship marks a distinction between members and outsiders based on their different relations to particular states.

Free movement within state territories and the right to readmission to this territory has become a hallmark of modern citizenship. Yet, in the international arena citizenship serves as a control device that strictly limits state obligations towards foreigners and permits governments to keep them out, or remove them, from their jurisdiction. A migration perspective highlights the boundaries of citizenship and political control over entry and exit as well as the fact that foreign residents remain in most countries deprived of the core rights of political participation.

These exclusionary aspects of citizenship raise some difficult problems for the theory of democracy. Such questions are often ignored in discussions that start from the false assumption that liberal democracies have already achieved full political inclusion and equality and focus then only on questions of social equality, economic opportunities, political participation and cultural liberties among citizens. As Joseph Carens has put it: 'Citizenship in the modern world is a lot like feudal status in the medieval world. It is assigned at birth; for the most part it is not subject to change by the individual's will and efforts; and it has a major impact upon that person's life chances' (Carens 1992: 26).[2]

The conceptual field of citizenship can be roughly outlined by distinguishing three dimensions. These are, first, citizenship as a political and legal status, second, legal rights and duties attached to this status, and, third, individual practices, dispositions and identities attributed to, or expected from those who hold the status. On each of these dimensions specific questions arise that are relevant for the study of migration and immigrant integration.

Citizenship status

Citizenship and nationality

From an international perspective, citizenship can be understood as a sorting device for allocating human populations to sovereign states. Under international law, the relation between states and their citizens is a legal bond that must be respected by other states and that entails certain duties between states, such as the obligation to readmit a person to the state whose citizen he or she is. International law also supports the right of states to determine under their domestic law who their citizens are. A principle of self-determination applied to citizenship inevitably creates conflicts between states over persons that are either claimed by no state or by more than one. Several international conventions deal with statelessness and multiple citizenship as areas of concern for the international community. Apart from addressing these intrinsic problems of self-determination, international law also tries to ensure that state practices in the determination of citizenship do not conflict with human rights norms regarding gender equality, racial discrimination, the status of children and of refugees.

In international law citizenship is generally called nationality. This is a somewhat ambiguous term, since in many languages it is also used for membership of an ethno-national group that need not be established as an independent state. In a related sense, the concept is also used for distinguishing states composed of several 'nationalities' from nation states. Unless otherwise stated, this report will not use the term nationality in this sense. We treat citizenship and nationality not as synonymous but as two sides of the same coin. Nationality refers to the international and external aspects of the relation between an individual and a sovereign state, whereas citizenship pertains to the internal aspects of this relation that are regulated by domestic law.

Citizenship is, however, also a much thicker concept than nationality in the strictly legal sense.[3] It is, on the one hand, wider in its scope, since it may refer to different types of political communities within and beyond independent states. On the other hand, it is also somewhat narrower because its normative connotations of membership in a self-governing community do not easily apply to regimes that lack appropriate institutions of popular government and can be characterised as non-self-governing. In other words, authoritarian states rule over their nationals, but these nationals can be called citizens only in a very limited sense.

Nationality as a device for regulating territorial movement

Migration is a form of human mobility that involves crossing territorial borders and taking up residence in another municipality, region, or country. In the contemporary world, most such geographic entities are organised as jurisdictions with precisely defined political borders. Some of these territorial borders are completely open for migration; some operate as funnels that permit a free flow in only one direction (entry or exit). The borders of municipalities and provinces are generally open within democratic states. Free internal movement is today not merely conceived as a right of citizens but as a human right. Once they have been admitted into the country, immigrants have the same right as native citizens to move around in search for better opportunities. This is clearly a modern liberal norm that was absent in earlier regimes, and it is still not fully respected in contemporary ones. For example, in Switzerland, residence permits of foreign nationals are generally valid only for a particular canton. In China, internal movement is severely restricted not only for foreign nationals but for citizens, too. All sovereign states, on the other hand, claim a right to control their borders. There is a human right of free exit, which is, again, not respected by most authoritarian regimes (Dowty 1987), but there is no corresponding right of migrants to enter the territory of another state. In this respect, citizenship operates as a filtering device in two basic ways. First, states are obliged to (re)admit their own nationals to their territory. These include nationals born abroad who have inherited their parents' citizenship. Second, states may impose specific restrictions on certain nationals (e.g. through visa requirements) while opening their borders for others (such as European Union citizens migrating to other Member States).

> Co-ethnic immigration preferences have been insufficiently studied.

Several states (among others Israel, Italy, Japan, Germany, Greece, Spain and Portugal) have also adopted preferences for foreign nationals whom they consider as part of a larger ethnic nation or as cultural and linguistic relatives who will more easily integrate in the destination country. These policies identify certain groups of non-citizens as potential citizens already before entering the territory. With some notable exceptions (e.g. Thränhardt 2000, Levy & Weiss 2002, Münz & Ohliger 2003, Joppke 2005), ethnic immigration preferences are a rather neglected topic in comparative migration research. This may partly be due to the fact that co-ethnic immigration does not fit well into dominant migration theories that focus on economic push and pull factors and on the sociology of migration networks. From these perspectives, it is not easy to understand why states would encourage the immigration of co-ethnics who crowd out other migrants with better skills and – in the German, Israeli and Japanese case – are sometimes not even familiar with the destination states' language. There is also a normative puzzle, which has not been fully explored, concerning the legitimacy of such distinctions. In the 1960s and 1970s, the exclusion of particular ethnic and racial groups from immigration was abandoned in the US, Canada and Australia and is now also regarded as illegitimate in European immigration states. The question whether preferential admission on similar grounds, which is still widespread and potentially growing, also amounts to discrimination, is disputed and has not been fully addressed yet. Migration research must be combined with studies of nation-building and nationalism for explaining the persistence of such preferential treatment as well as for evaluating it.

Membership, ties and belonging

Citizenship is not only a device for sorting out desirable and undesirable immigrants; it also establishes a second gate that migrants have to pass in order to become full members of the polity. As a membership status, citizenship has certain features distinguishing it from related concepts that describe various forms of affiliation between individuals and territorially bounded societies.

There is emerging literature on modes of belonging that focuses on migrants' constructions of their own identities in relation to different places, groups and countries (e.g. Christiansen & Hedetoft 2004, Rummens 2003, Sicakkan & Lithman 2004). Seen from a different angle, such affiliations may be called ties or stakes. The notion of migrants' social, cultural, economic and political ties focuses our attention less on identities and more on social relations and practices that can be directly observed and that structure individual lives.[4] Such ties may be called 'stakes' once we consider them as linking individual interests with those of other persons and communities, including large-scale political communities.

Of these three modes of affiliation, 'belonging' is the most flexible and open-ended one. Migrants may not only develop a sense of belonging to several societies, regions, cities, ethnic and cultural traditions or religious and political movements; they can also feel to belong to imagined communities located in a distant past or future. Modes of belonging will, however, not be purely subjectively defined since they always refer to some socially constructed entity and are shaped by discourses within these about who belongs and who does not. Migrating between distinct societies also creates multiple social ties and political and economic stakes, but, different from their sense of belonging, these must be grounded in some factual dependency of an individual's activities and opportunities on her or his affiliations.

Citizenship is a more discriminating concept than both ties and belonging because it is a status of membership granted by an established or aspiring political community. Citizenship is neither a purely subjective phenomenon (as is a sense of belonging) nor is it objective in the sense that it can be inferred from external observation of a person's social circumstances and activities. Citizenship is instead based on a quasi-contractual relation between an individual and a collectivity. In contrast with belonging and ties, membership is also a binary concept rather than one that allows for gradual changes. Citizenship marks a boundary between insiders and outsiders. This boundary may be permeable or impermeable, it may be stable or shifting, and it may be clearly marked or become somewhat blurred. But it is always recognisable as a threshold. If you cross it, your status, rights and obligations in relation to a political community change as a consequence.

These considerations point to two different tasks for research. There is an agenda for empirical research on 'misalignments' (Sicakkan & Lithman 2004, Hampshire 2005) between citizenship, ties and belong-

> We need to study mismatches between citizenship, ties and belonging as
> well as institutional reforms that may reduce these.

ing; and there is a task for comparative as well as normative legal and political analysis of political institutions and practices that examines how migrants' multiple and shifting affiliations are taken into account in determining their membership status (see e.g. Castles & Davidson 2000).

In an influential analysis of membership rules in liberal states, Michael Walzer (1983) has drawn analogies with families, clubs or neighbourhoods. States behave like families when they automatically confer their citizenship by descent and if they give preference to co-ethnic immigrants; they are like clubs in discretionary naturalisation of those who are expected to contribute to the common good of the polity; and they are like open neighbourhoods if they give citizenship to all born in the territory or if they extend equal rights to all residents. From a normative perspective, Walzer defends state rights to control immigration along those criteria suggested by the analogy with families and clubs but insists that the gate to citizenship status must be open to all permanent residents. Excluding settled immigrants from access to full citizenship amounts to political tyranny (Walzer 1983: 62), since it subjects a part of the permanent population to legislation without representation. Many contemporary theorists of democracy support a basic norm of inclusion along these lines. Robert Dahl, for example, postulates that 'the *demos* must include all adult members of the association except transients and persons proved to be mentally defective' (Dahl 1989: 129). This leaves open where to draw the line between transients and permanent members and whether to include settled immigrants through an extension of rights or through naturalisation.

Any such norm of inclusion constrains the receiving polity's options to exclude permanent resident immigrants from citizenship or to admit them only selectively. The club analogy suggests a quite different approach that affirms these as legitimate policy options. Along these lines, some public choice economists have recently analysed citizenship as a 'club good'. Club goods are different from public goods, such as clean air or national security, from whose consumption no one can be excluded, because access to a club good depends on membership. The economic theory of club goods, as developed first by James Buchanan (1965), suggests that rationally acting clubs accept new members as long as benefits from their financial contributions or positive externalities exceed costs to the present members, such as integration costs or crowding out effects with regard to the use of club goods (Straubhaar

2003).[5] This argument is, however, more plausible for immigration control than for naturalisation (Jordan & Düvell 2003). The economic rationale for controlling access to citizenship depends on the relative benefits attached to this status compared to that of foreign nationals. As we will discuss below, large gaps between these two statuses have become less common than they used to be in the past. Nevertheless, this is not an irreversible trend, and economic arguments for rationing access to citizenship may eventually become stronger.

Comparative trends with regard to rules of access and loss of citizenship are extensively discussed in chapter 2 of this report. However, there is a more general puzzle about these rules that has been recently addressed by some legal and political theorists. What justification is there for distinguishing between automatic acquisition at birth and naturalisation regarded as a contract based on active consent by both the immigrant and the receiving polity? Why should immigrants have to apply for naturalisation rather than being granted automatic access to this status after some time of residence?[6] Ruth Rubio-Marín (2000) has suggested that the imperative of democratic inclusion would justify making acquisition of citizenship by immigrants automatic under the condition that they have a right to retain their previous nationality. Dora Kostakopoulou (2003) argues that naturalisation is altogether an outdated institution that should be replaced by automatic civic registration based on residence and conditional on absence of criminal record. Other authors object that automatic ius domicili was a historic practice in some monarchical regimes that relied on the idea of subjecthood without consent. Naturalising foreign nationals against their will may not only infringe on their individual freedom of choice between alternative legal statuses but also on the rights of states of origin to protect their nationals abroad (Bauböck 2004a). Finally, native citizens may expect that newcomers who have ties to other countries publicly declare their intention to join the political community before they can fully participate in its collective decision-making process.

Such observations reflect, however, the reality of the current nation-state system rather than a general necessity of self-governing communities to control the admission of newcomers to their membership. At the substate level, regional citizenship in autonomous provinces of federal states or local citizenship in municipalities is automatically acquired through residence. At the supranational European level, control over admission to Union citizenship rests with the Member States rather than the EU itself.[7]

Contemporary studies on citizenship in migration contexts have focused on modes of acquisition through ius sanguinis, ius soli or naturalisation rather than on ways of losing citizenship through voluntary renunciation, automatic expiration or involuntary withdrawal. The

> There is more research on rules of admission than on loss of citizenship.
> Yet policies on withdrawal and renunciation also structure migrants' choices
> and vary widely across states.

agenda for comparative analyses of citizenship loss will be discussed in chapter 2 of this report. From a normative perspective, there is, on the one hand, little consensus on whether immigrants' admission to citizenship should be automatic, an option that can be freely chosen, or a discretionary decision of the state. On the other hand, liberal theorists agree that emigrants ought to be released from citizenship upon request. A considerable number of states, however, still assert the old doctrine of perpetual allegiance (see text box 2 on page 49). Other aspects of citizenship loss have been much less discussed in the literature: Should individuals be allowed to renounce the citizenship of their country of permanent residence under the condition that they acquire another nationality, e.g. through marrying a foreign national? Should states also have a right to deprive their citizen residents of nationality under similar circumstances? Should ius sanguinis transmission of citizenship abroad be limited to one or two generations? Or should those who have been born outside the country and have acquired citizenship through descent lose it unless they 'return' to their country of citizenship before the age of majority? While the analogy with voluntary associations endorses an unconditional right to free exit, the notion of stakeholdership in a democratic polity suggests strict limits for involuntary as well as voluntary loss of citizenship among residents and might also be usefully explored in answering questions about legitimate withdrawal and retention outside the territorial jurisdiction.

Citizenship rights and duties

Typologies of citizenship rights

The general status of citizenship can be further differentiated in terms of the individual rights that it entails. A classification proposed by the constitutional lawyer Georg Jellinek (1892) is in many ways still useful today. Jellinek distinguishes a negative status of liberty that entails mere freedom from unlawful coercion from a positive status that implies a duty by the state to promote the interests of individuals through a system of public rights and an active status that entitles its holders to participate, or be represented in, democratic institutions. A similar typology, but with a different sequence derived from a historical theory about the evolution of citizenship, is proposed by T. H. Marshall in his 1949 lectures on social citizenship and class (Marshall 1965). In this account the earliest elements of citizenship are civil rights that correspond to the institution of independent courts. These are supplemented in a second stage with political rights associated with the rise of parliamentary sovereignty. The third and most recent element is social citizenship that starts with public schooling but is only fully developed in the post World War II European welfare state.

Marshall's essay triggered a whole new literature on citizenship. Key issues in this discussion were: the question whether social citizenship should be seen as strengthening the egalitarian ethos implicit in the general idea or rather as weakening active political citizenship through passive dependency on the welfare state; a critique of the underlying evolutionary theory that did not fit the pattern in several continental European states where social citizenship had preceded political participation rights or where citizenship developed in a less gradual way as a result of historic upheavals and regime changes; and a debate whether Marshall's list needed to be supplemented by more recent emphases on environmental and cultural citizenship rights.

Citizenship rights of non-citizen residents

The debate on Marshall's analytical model has also raised interesting questions for migration research. A first question concerns foreign nationals' access to the three bundles of citizenship rights. Even irregular migrants can formally claim certain basic rights of civil citizenship that are considered human rights, e.g. due process rights in court or elementary social rights, such as emergency health care or public schooling for their children. On the one hand, these rights are obviously precarious since they effectively depend on a right to residence and because most states of immigration accept only few constraints on their discretionary powers of deportation and expulsion of migrants in an irregular status. On the other hand, regularisation measures have been frequent in all Mediterranean EU states and have also been occasionally implemented in traditional immigration states, such as France or the USA.

Immigrants in a regular status have access to additional rights. On the civil rights dimension, freedom of speech, association and assembly was strongly restricted for foreign nationals in most democratic countries before World War II. There are remaining limitations in certain states concerning political activities, e.g. public demonstrations or the right to form political parties and to sit on their boards. However, by and large, core civil rights have been extended to legal foreign residents, again with the important exception of migration-related rights such as protection against expulsion, the right to return from abroad, and family reunification in the country of residence.

Inclusion of legal immigrants into means-tested programmes of social citizenship is still partial and reversible

The most significant inclusion of foreign nationals has probably occurred with regard to social citizenship. In democratic states with a longer history of immigration, there is nowadays comparatively little legal exclusion of foreign nationals in the provision of public education, health and housing and with regard to financial benefits such as social insurance payments in case of unemployment, sickness, work accidents or retirement. This is very different in needs-based and means-tested public welfare systems where foreign nationals are frequently excluded or receive reduced benefits. The rationale behind this discrimination is that immigrants are supposed to be either self-supporting or to be supported by their sponsors. In contrast with virtually all other citizenship rights, inclusion of migrants into social citizenship is also not an irreversible process. In the 1990s legal residents in the US and in Australia have been deprived of welfare benefits (Aleinikoff 2000, Zappala & Castles 2000).[8] In a broader conception of social citizenship, one should include not merely legal equality of public entitlements but also protection against discriminiation in employment, housing, education and health. The two anti-discrimination directives of the European Union, which will be discussed in chapter 3, have obliged Member States to expand and harmonise their policies in this area without, however, covering disrimination on grounds of third country nationality. An even more substantive conception of social citizenship would look at unequal rates of poverty or opportunities for upward social mobility. In this respect, the gaps in achieving full social citizenship for immigrants are obviously still very large.

Political participation and representation is the dimension of citizenship from which foreign nationals remain generally excluded. However, even in this area we find patterns of partial inclusion. In the US an alien franchise was very widespread at state level until World War I. Today, non-citizens cannot vote in the US, in Canada and Australia, but they do enjoy active voting rights even in national elections in New Zealand. Several Latin American countries also do not require national citizenship for the vote. In Europe, the UK grants full voting rights to Irish and Commonwealth citizens. Another significant European development is the emergence of a 'residential citizenship' at municipal level that is disconnected from nation-state membership. Thirteen of the 25 Member States of the EU now grant the local franchise to all foreigners who meet residence requirements (see table 2 in the annex). Additionally, all EU citizens residing in another Member State enjoy the franchise in local and European Parliament elections. This development may be interpreted as a gradual emancipation of local citizenship from state citizenship, with the former becoming more open than the latter for the inclusion of immigrants (see Aleinikoff & Klusmeyer 2002, chapter 3).

> Legal incorporation of foreign residents can be measured by comparing their rights across immigration countries. Indicators should allow for ranking states as well as measuring convergence and progress over time.

Comparative analyses of the rights of foreign nationals that go beyond documenting legal developments are still rare. Based on a comprehensive legal comparison of six European countries (Davy 2001), Harald Waldrauch (2001) has developed an index of obstacles for the legal integration of foreign nationals that measures how inclusive or discriminatory the legislation on foreign residents is in different policy areas in each country. Unfortunately, this study has not been updated or extended to other countries. The Brussels-based Migration Policy Group has initiated a comparative project on 'Benchmarking citizenship policies' (British Council 2005). A comprehensive and reliable set of standardised indicators for citizenship inclusion of migrants could be of great importance for researchers and policy makers alike. Ideally, these indicators should be applied to a large sample of countries and be updated each year. This would permit not only ranking countries but also measuring convergence and divergence across time as well as progress with regard to equality and inclusion within each country and for specific sets of rights. The methodological hurdles for standardised comparison of different country's legislations on foreign nationals are formidable but not insurmountable. It would be desirable, but much more difficult, to also include information on the implementation of laws and sociological indicators for migrants' actual access to rights.

Such comparative studies on migrants' access to citizenship and rights as foreign residents allow the testing of two widespread assumptions that we may call the convergence and liberalisation hypotheses. The convergence hypothesis claims that citizenship policies of democratic countries of immigration are moving closer to each other. This might be explained as a result of first, spontaneous policy transfers through learning from successful examples, second, integration into international and supranational institutions, such as the Council of Europe and the European Union, which then develop a harmonisation agenda with regard to citizenship policies and, third, globalisation that increases interdependencies between states, limits their sovereignty and exposes them to similar immigration flows from a growing diversity of origins. The liberalisation hypothesis asumes furthermore that this convergence is moving towards more liberal standards of inclusion. This direction has been attributed either to the emergence of a global human rights discourse and regime (Soysal 1994) or to the growing impact of constitutional courts that share interpretations of legal norms across national boundaries (Joppke 2001). The secular trend of extending citizenship rights in Western democracies to long-term foreign residents has led Tomas Hammar (1990) to suggest that a distinct status of 'denizenship' has emerged between temporary residence and full citizenship. This claim has triggered a debate that will be addressed in chapter 2 of this report. The convergence and liberalisation hypotheses have so far been generally tested based on anecdotal evidence from a limited number of case studies. A much more comprehensive and methodologically sophisticated approach is needed.

While there are many studies on migrant denizenship, less research has been carried out on other forms of 'quasi-citizenship' that are not based on residence but on special bilateral relations with other states or on cultural and ethnic preferences for certain immigrants. The most prominent example of this is, of course, European Union citizenship, which will also be discussed in chapter 3. Other cases include Commonwealth citizens in the UK, Nordic citizens in the Nordic states and Latin Americans in the Iberic peninsula.

In the 1990s citizenship debates in political theory have strongly focused on the cultural dimension that is neglected in Marshall's approach because he assumes a homogenous national culture as a background. Various scholars, among them Iris Young (1990), Jeff Spinner-Halev (1994), Will Kymlicka (1995), Veit Bader (1997), Jacob Levy (2000), Bhikhu Parekh (2000), have extensively discussed cultural claims and rights of immigrant minorities, often by comparing them to the claims of indigenous peoples and territorially concentrated national minorities. This important dimension of citizenship will not be discussed in this report since it is the topic of a separate thematic IMISCOE cluster (B6).

The migration-citizenship nexus generates questions not only about immigrants' access to rights but also about the impact of immigration on the citizenship regime of the destination country. For example, there is a long tradition of studies on the impact of the 'ethnic vote' in the US. This concern, which can be safely predicted to grow also in European states with large numbers of naturalised immigrants, will be discussed in chapter 4. Other literature focuses on the impact of immigration on welfare regimes, the balance between contributions paid and benefits received by migrants, and the sustainability of welfare-state regulation of working conditions or wages in case of large scale immigration. These mostly economic analyses are addressed in other thematic clusters of our network (B4 and B5). From a citizenship perspective, Ewald Engelen (2003) has recently argued that the tension between high levels of social protection in European welfare regimes and openness for newcomers can be mitigated through a pluralistic regime of differentiated rights combined with flexible enforcement.

External and transnational citizenship

While there is a substantial body of theoretical literature and of empirical case studies on migrants' access to rights in destination countries, much less attention has been devoted to external citizenship rights that migrants enjoy in their countries of origin. These include minimally the right to return and to diplomatic protection. Sending states differ with regard to property rights concerning inheritance and property in land, which are of particular importance for migrants who want to keep their return options open. Finally, external citizenship may also include certain welfare benefits, cultural support and the right to vote. A growing number of sending states have introduced absentee ballots and some (among them Colombia and Italy) have even reserved seats in parliament for the expatriate constituency (Itzigsohn 2000, Bauböck 2003a). Long-distance voting raises a number of normative problems. Should expatriates be represented in parliaments whose legislation will not apply to them? Should they have a vote even if they have not been exposed to public debates about the candidates and issues? A stakeholder approach to citizenship may allow affirmative answers for those migrants whose ongoing ties to their 'homelands' involve them deeply in its present political life and future destiny (Bauböck 2003a). The lack of comparative and normative studies on external citizenship rights is a major gap in current research. Closing it is also important from a 'receiving state' citizenship perspective since sending-state policies in this area are a major factor determining immigrants' choices between return migration, permanent settlement as a foreign resident, and naturalisation.

> The lack of comparative and normative studies on external citizenship rights is a major gap in current research.

Relations between migrants and countries, regions or local communities of origin have been at the centre of studies on transnational migration. In its broadest sense, this term signals a paradigm change in migration research from a traditional approach of regarding migration as a unidirectional movement that ends with settlement and assimilation in the destination society. Transnational migration studies emphasise instead: that migration is often a process of going back and forth several times between different countries, that even immigrants who are long-term residents may retain strong ties to countries of origin and participate in these countries' developments, e.g. by sending home remittances, and that also sedentary populations who never migrate themselves participate in transnational networks and activities when they are linked to migrants through family and ethnic networks. The Oxford-based transnational communities project, led by Steven Vertovec, and several other scholars (e.g. Glick Schiller, Basch & Blanc-Szanton 1995, Pries 1997, Faist 2000, Portes 2001, Levitt 2001, Nyberg-Sørensen & Olwig 2002, Guarnizo 2003) have established migrant transnationalism as an important and growing field of theoretical and empirical research.

Claims about the importance of this phenomenon are, however, disputed by scholars who emphasise, on the one hand, that transnationalism is not a historically new phenomenon[9] and, on the other hand, that active involvement in transnational practices may be quite limited among first generation migrants and will gradually fade away over subsequent generations. Rogers Brubaker (2001) has identified a 'return of assimilation' in French public discourses, in German public policies and in American academic research. However, authors like Brubaker or Richard Alba and Victor Nee (2003) use a rather sophisticated concept of assimilation that has been clearly enriched by the transnationalism debate and deviates from common usage of the term in public debates.

> Empirical research on transnational citizenship should study how migrants combine, or choose between political identities and statuses and how citizenship policies of states impact on each other.

Political theorists who have combined the concepts of transnationalism and citizenship have interpreted the term transnationalism in a somewhat broader sense than most of the sociological and anthropological literature (Bauböck 1994, Kleger 1997). Transnational citizenship refers not only to migrants' political activities directed towards their countries of origin but also to institutional changes and new conceptions of citizenship in states linked to each other through migration chains. Transnational citizenship may be described as overlapping memberships between separate territorial jurisdictions that blur their political boundaries to a certain extent. This phenomenon includes external citizenship rights in states of origin, denizenship and cultural minority rights in states of migrant settlement, and multiple nationality. Transnational citizenship is an analytic concept that has often been associated with post-national approaches. The latter suggest that migration and other phenomena of globalisation undermine the political significance of nation states and their boundaries (Glick Schiller, Basch & Blanc-Szanton 1994, Soysal 1994, Jacobson 1996). Transnational citizenship is, however, still about migrants' affiliations with distinct and clearly bounded political communities. Empirical research in this field ought to study, on the one hand, how migrants combine, or choose between various political identities and statuses and, on the other hand, how the policies of the states involved impact on each other.

> Research on immigrant communities must study under which conditions legitimate religious and political transnationalism becomes linked to dangerous fanaticism and radicalism.

Within the broad field of transnational studies, specific emphasis has been placed by some authors on the notion of diasporic identities and citizenship. The term diaspora is defined in quite different ways in the literature (Cohen 1997, Vertovec 2000). We suggest that diasporic identities and practices refer to a specific kind of transnationalism characterised by its persistence across several generations, by strong networks and shared identities between communities dispersed across several 'host states', and, most importantly, by a shared mission to build, or fundamentally transform, a political or religious homeland community. Diasporic citizenship provides therefore a much stronger basis for political mobilisation than other kinds of transnational linkages. Often, it is driven by an unfinished nation-building project in support of which expatriates are rallied. Alternatively, it may emerge from strong solidarity among religious communities dispersed across different countries. The Jewish diaspora before the Zionist nation-building project and the contemporary revival of ideas about a global Islamic umma illustrate such manifestations of religious diaspora. A sense of belonging to a religious diaspora may remain confined to the spiritual realm and pastoral linkages between dispersed communities. But under conditions of social marginalisation and politicisation of religious differences it may also trigger transnational political activism, and eventually political radicalism. Studying these conditions and drawing the line between legitimate forms of religious and political transnationalism and dangerous radicalism is an important topic for research.

Duties of non-citizen residents

In republican theories of citizenship, rights are always connected with duties. However, as T. H. Marshall already observed, there is a 'changing balance between rights and duties. Rights have been multiplied, and they are precise' (Marshall 1965: 129). By contrast, legal duties are either very general (the duty to obey the law) or few and specific rather than universal. Compulsory education is the most universal among citizenship duties, paying taxes depends on income, military service has historically been a male duty only and is currently abolished in more and more democratic states, jury service is a duty that only few citizens ever have to fulfil.

Are there specific patterns how such duties apply to non-citizen immigrants? Duties of education and paying taxes or social security contributions are not attached to nationality but to residence, income and employment. By contrast, military and jury service are generally regarded as linked to citizenship status since these duties have historically been at the very core of ancient and early modern notions of citizenship. Even this is, however, not a universal pattern. Although international law does not allow forcing foreign nationals into the army, permanent residents in the US would be liable to perform military service if the government decided to reintroduce the draft.

Citizenship duties are thus applied to migrants in a less gradual and differentiated way than citizenship rights. Yet, receiving countries have periodically asserted a specific duty of immigrants to assimilate or integrate and have used the naturalisation process as an occasion for asserting a duty of loyalty that remains at best implicit for native citizens. Austria, Germany, Denmark, Finland, the Netherlands and Sweden have introduced publicly funded integration courses for newcomers that consist mainly of language training with some additional practical orientation and information on the legal and political system of the receiving country. Initially, participation in such courses was generally voluntary, but there is now a shift towards mandatory participation and financing through fees. Sanctions for non-participation range from fines to loss of welfare benefits and ultimately even of residence permits. The Netherlands have recently even extended the duty to learn the host country's language to family members abroad who apply for reunification. These are asked to pass a language test before entering Dutch territory.

Government institutions in the states concerned have commissioned comparative studies on the experience in other countries or evaluation reports where such programmes have been in place for some time (e.g. Entzinger 2004, Michalowski 2004). There is also new literature in political theory on language rights that addresses the normative question whether or how immigrants should be forced to learn the language of the receiving society (Kymlicka & Patten 2003, Bauböck 2003b). What is missing so far are policy analyses that explain this significant shift and new orientation in integration policies in European states.

Citizenship virtues and practices

Republican theorists from Aristotle, Cicero, Machiavelli and Rousseau to the present have always emphasised that citizenship is not only about legal status, rights and duties but also about civic virtues that are necessary in order to sustain self-government over time. In contrast with legal duties, civic virtues may be defined as the disposition of citizens to regard the common good of the polity as an important part of their own interests. Civic virtues range from habitual participation in elections to what may be called heroic virtues of civil disobedience against unjust laws or the readiness to fight in defending one's polity against tyranny or external aggression. In large representative liberal democracies whose citizens experience political institutions as rather remote, discourses about civic virtue are often regarded as outdated and somewhat suspicious as they can easily lead to pressure for conformism and hostility towards outsiders. In contemporary Europe, republican rhetoric about the need for shared values and loyalty towards constitutional principles is, indeed, more often invoked in response to perceived threats from immigration and cultural and religious diversity than in response to political passivity or xenophobic attitudes among native citizens. Political theorists have occasionally entered these debates (Kymlicka & Norman 1994, Van Gunsteren 1998, Oldfield 1990, Pettit 1997, Bauböck 2002).

A more important agenda for research emerges from empirically studying citizenship practices among migrant populations. These include participation in elections, running for public office, political mobilisation for specific issues, forming associations and joining interest groups and political parties. In a transnational perspective, such practices should be studied both in relation to countries of settlement and of origin. Chapter 4 discusses this research agenda extensively. There are important tasks in this area for quantitative research based on statistical data and surveys that include large enough migrant samples, but there is an even stronger need for qualitative research. Focus group discussions could be a particularly well-suited research instrument for exploring migrants' self-interpretation of citizenship practices in a setting that allows for deliberation and the formation of group attitudes.

2 The legal status of immigrants and their access to nationality

Albert Kraler

The legal status of foreign nationals

In Europe, the legal framework governing the statuses of foreign nationals has undergone radical changes in the past one and a half decades or so, and it continues to evolve. The formal introduction of European Union citizenship (see chapter 3) with the 1992 Maastricht Treaty, the continuing expansion of (mobility) rights enjoyed by EU citizens, the development of a common EU status for long term residents from third countries as well as the definition of rights to family reunion tied to that status (see text box 6 in chapter 3) – all these developments suggest a continuous expansion of rights enjoyed by non-nationals as well as a narrowing of the gap between citizens' rights 'at home' and outside their country of nationality. Looked at more closely, however, actual developments are much more complex and contradictory than the narrative of a progressive expansion of 'citizenship rights for non-citizens' suggests. What we find instead are different outcomes for different legal categories of migrants.[1]

Long before the harmonisation of immigrant policy at EU level, Tomas Hammar's influential study *Democracy and the Nation State* (1990) noted a significant convergence of European states' immigrant policies with respect to the rights granted to permanent foreign residents. Hammar observed that long-term immigrants more often than not enjoyed a relatively secure residence status as well as other rights, for example equal access to welfare entitlements and sometimes even political rights. This led him to conclude that in fact a new status has emerged, which he called 'denizenship'. Hammar's primary focus was to defend denizenship from a normative perspective, interpreting it as a sensible alternative to citizenship for first generation migrants (see chapter 1). This point was taken up by Yasemin Soysal (1994) who interpreted the emergence of denizenship as an indication of the decline of nationality and the rise of 'post-national citizenship' anchored in international human rights institutions rather than being tied to membership of a particular state, a view echoed by Saskia Sassen (1996) and others.

> Efforts to create a single status for long-term resident third country nationals in the EU conflict with new integration requirements imposed by some Member States.

The optimism of the 'globalist thesis', however, has since been subject to intense criticism (see for example Guiraudon & Lahav 2000, Hansen 2002, Joppke 1998). Empirically, the convergence of EU Member States' legislation in regard to the status of long-term resident third country nationals has been shown by Groenendijk, Guild & Barzilay (2000). This study also noted the early harmonising effects of the Association Treaty with Turkey, or more precisely, the EEC-Turkey Association Treaty Council Decision 1/80, on the status of Turkish nationals, and the impact it had on the rights of other (long-term resident) nationals (see also chapters 3 and 4). Precisely what kind of rights denizens may enjoy, however, is subject to considerable variation and is certainly worthy of further comparative analysis (see Kondo 2001, Gronendijk et al. 2000).

Text Box 1: Alexander I. Gray, Goizane Mota, Integration management in the Basque country: citizenship disconnected from nationality

For most nation-state governments, citizenship has traditionally been closely connected with the legal status of nationality. Political authorities at substate levels, however, sometimes use a broader conception of citizenship in order to strengthen their political intervention vis-à-vis the central state. An interesting example is the Immigration Plan, legitimised by the Basque government Council and officially adopted in December 2003, even though some measures were already enforced by the end of 2002. According to this document, a Basque citizen is someone who resides in the territory, that is to say, citizenship is regarded as unrelated to the person's nationality. Article 7.1 of the Autonomous Statute reads: 'For the purposes of this Statute, those who are registered as residents, in accordance with general State laws and in any of the integrated municipalities of the territory of the Autonomous Community, will have the status of Basque citizenship.' The only requirement to obtain Basque citizenship is to prove residency in a municipality, that is, to be registered in a town hall. According to Basque public policy, the civil, social and economic rights of the newly registered person are the same as those of a native person. It is important to note that legal nationality still falls under the competence of the Spanish government. Thus, in the case of non-European immigrants, official interventions (of which there are

> 215, as specified in the Plan) occur mainly in the area of social integration (education, labour, health, residence, access to services, etc.) where the Basque government has direct authority.
> The Immigration Plan defines integration as a dynamic and bi-directional process based on multilateral and reciprocal adaptation. Interculturality is the cornerstone that allows free development of diverse identities on an equal footing, and the interaction and interrelation amongst people with different identities.
> There are, however, constitutional limitations to making a purely residence-based citizenship in the Basque country fully effective. Taking into account that the right to vote and eligibility falls under the competence of the Spanish government, the Plan focuses on other methods of civic participation. At the same time, the Basque Parliament has urged the Spanish Government to derogate the Spanish Immigration Law and to replace it with one enjoying a broader and deeper consensus.

Reflecting the expansion of the EU's role in migration policy, the focus of the debate on denizenship, or in EU terminology, on a secure legal status of third country nationals largely shifted to the European level in the second half of the 1990s (see chapter 3). On the one hand, there is still a lot of variation or even new divergence concerning access to denizenship in the EU Member States. On the other hand, the European Union has taken considerable effort to harmonise this status and some of its ensuing rights.

> More research is needed on the various trajectories leading to the expansion of long-term resident migrants' rights in Europe and elsewhere.

But why and under what conditions did governments of most European states 'allow' the expansion of rights of long-term resident third country nationals in the first place? Recent works by Freeman (1998), Guiraudon (1998), Guiraudon & Lahav (2000) and Hansen (2002) point at some possible factors that help to explain this development. These include the influence of migrant lobby and advocacy groups, a judiciary relatively insulated from politics, path dependency (e.g. expansion of rights as a consequence of particularly strong constitutional provisions protecting the rights of individuals qua persons), the location and nature of 'policy venues' (i.e. whether policies are designed behind closed doors or in public fora; whether policy decisions are made in consensual or competitive arenas of policy making; whether policies are made/ implemented at national or lower levels of government or are 'privatised' altogether etc.), and the nature of the rights involved (e. g. with respect to the welfare system, differential inclusion in contributory or non-contributory systems of welfare benefits). While most of these hypotheses are plausible and empirically well-grounded, they have not yet been systematically tested against each other or been integrated into a more theoretical account.

One issue deserving more attention, in particular after the recent 'restrictonist' backlashes in several European immigration countries, is the relationship between immigration control and the legal status of foreign nationals. In this regard, several questions can be raised, for example, to what extent did the restriction of new immigration coincide with the expansion of rights of (long-term) resident migrants and was there a deliberate link between partial restriction and the expansion of rights of denizens? How and to what extent did governments try to reassert their powers to freely determine the status of immigrants, e.g. by raising the barriers to long-term denizenship? How did other stakeholders react to this? To what extent did international human rights institutions limit and influence government policies?

In Austria, for example, it could be argued that restrictionist policy reforms introduced in the early 1990s under the slogan 'integration before new immigration' also provided the terms on which legal discrimination of foreign residents could be effectively challenged. Thus, the improvement of the rights of long-term resident third country nationals in the course of the reform of aliens legislation in 1997 was to some degree only possible because the earlier reform had highlighted the precarious legal status of migrants already present in Austria and thus had unwittingly brought the issue of long-term foreign residents' rights to the centre of debate (Jawhari 2000).

> Migration control policies and reforms of the legal status of long-term foreign nationals often impact on each other in unexpected ways

Yet, governments did not simply acquiesce to the demands of pressure groups or to the expansion of legal rights by the judiciary. They found ways to circumvent constitutional and other limits to migration control, shifting responsibilities downward (to regional and local levels), upward (to intergovernmental fora), and outward (to private actors such as transport enterprises, security companies, employers and others) (Guiraudon & Lahav 2000). In the new Member States, on the other hand, some of which host significant migrant minorities, the legal framework governing immigration matters heavily drew on models from Western Europe (e.g. in the Czech Republic and the Baltic States). However, this adoption of supposedly liberal models of migration control resulted in quite different outcomes, depending very much on the target groups of the reforms and the policy issues involved. In the Baltic States with their large Russian minorities, international organisations such as the Council of Europe, the OSCE and, through its 1993 Copenhagen criteria, the European Union significantly influenced legislation (Barrington 2000, Day & Shaw 2003, Vermeersch 2002, 2003, 2004).

Assessing how international human rights norms shape domestic immigrant policies more generally, however, is more difficult and has been a relatively neglected area of research. A recent study by Guiraudon & Lahav (2000) concludes that even though the European Convention for the Protection of Human Rights and Fundamental Freedoms (ECHR) has been increasingly invoked in the 1990s to challenge national immigration legislation, the reasons why lawyers and judges alike challenge national policies by means of international law have more to do with national constitutional politics than with the existence of international human rights institutions. These scholars thus give an explanation radically different from that offered by 'globalists', such as Soysal (1994), Jacobson (1996) or Sassen (1996).

The attention devoted to the study of the status of permanent foreign residents has also somewhat diluted the fact that, empirically, there are a multitude of different statuses that an alien might possess. These include the rather paradoxical statuses irregular migrants acquire when they present themselves to the authorities to claim asylum and their claims are rejected or when they are apprehended by police agencies, and in both cases are deemed undeportable for reasons of non-refoulement or lack of identity documents. While such irregular migrants often remain in the territory of the respective states for rather long periods, most European countries have generally been reluctant to open up any of the three 'entry gates' described by Hammar (1990: 9ff) (temporary residence, permanent residence, naturalisation) to partial or full membership in host societies, leaving these migrants in a state of limbo for an indefinite period.[2]

Moreover, the recent re-introduction of temporary workers' programmes in Austria and Germany (in Austria more so than in the German case) explicitly exclude access to permanent residence status for foreign nationals so admitted. This raises the question how access to permanent residence status is regulated and how governments effectively deny such migrants any chances to improve their legal status and to gain eventually full membership rights (see Menz 2002). To be sure, across Europe, long-term residents now, by and large, possess a reasonably secure residence status as well as a range of other rights and benefits, often denied to short-term migrants. However, as governments are reasserting control over immigration, control over access to denizenship increasingly seems to become a crucial building block of immigration policies. For example, to be granted a permanent residence permit may hinge upon continuous residence in the country, and, perhaps more importantly, on the continuous possession of a renewable short-term permit. It may thus exclude a significant proportion of migrants who have in principle resided in the country for the duration set out by law but are unable to meet the specific legal requirements.[3] In the future, this discretion of governments in controlling access to denizenship will be reduced but not fully eliminated by the implementation of the Community directive on the status of long-term residents (Directive EC (2003) 109) (see also the second section of chapter 3).

> The concept of 'civic stratification' highlights the diversity of rights and legal statuses foreign nationals may enjoy.

Migration scholars have frequently noted that the term 'foreign national' is not a meaningful category of social analysis. They have, however, largely neglected the fact that the term is not a consistent legal category either. On a general level, the rights of EU/EEA nationals (and Swiss nationals) in Europe differ markedly from those of third country nationals. But third country nationals have various legal statuses, too – depending on the grounds, 'legality' and duration of their stay. Thus, there is an increasing differentiation, if not fragmentation of legal statuses for foreigners, which Eleonore Kofmann (2002) and Lydia Morris (2001a,b, 2003) described as 'civic stratification', borrowing a term suggested by David Lockwood (1996).

Civic stratification, the law as a source of discrimination, and gender

In his 1996 essay on civic stratification, David Lockwood argued that inequalities of class not only affect how citizenship (or denizenship for that matter) is designed. Citizenship itself (or any other legal status) may also be an important factor in exacerbating social inequalities and producing new cleavages. In regard to immigration policy, however, few studies have been undertaken that would explicitly try to analyse the consequences of immigration law on migrants' social status, social mobility, development of social capital, etc. As a result, research on civic stratification has almost exclusively focused on a normative and descriptive level. Similarly, the fact that immigration laws themselves may lead to social and economic inequalities, and thus constitute important sources of discrimination, has largely remained taboo in the emerging debate on anti-discrimination policies in the EU and elsewhere.[4] Yet immigration regulations do significantly constrain the freedom of choice of (new) immigrants and thus have important consequences for social freedom at large, for example by restricting the right to change employers or the occupation one may have as well as access to social benefits or to other employment related rights, or by excluding some categories of migrants from employment altogether. It is evident that restrictions of employment rights have important consequences for labour relations. Similarly, specific conditions imposed on persons admitted through family reunification procedures in some states (e.g. exclusion from employment, linkage of the right to stay to the primary permit holder) may create an enormous dependency on the primary permit holder and thus result in a higher vulnerability to abuse and other adverse consequences. As the majority of migrants admitted through family reunion procedures tend to be women, important gender issues are involved, e.g. whether divorce automatically leads to the cessation of the permit, whether independent permits may be granted in case of abusive relationships etc.

> The consequences of different legal statuses for the social status of non-nationals, their social mobility and vulnerability to discrimination have been hardly studied at all.

The directive on the status of long-term residents may improve access to denizenship, but it will not end 'civic stratification', as states will still have considerable leeway to exclude certain categories of migrants from access to denizenship. These are in particular irregular migrants, migrants who enter a country on non-renewable short-term permits but often are de facto long-term circular migrants[5], and other migrants on short-term permits for specific purposes who are normally not eligible for long-term permits (for example students). In only a few countries reliable empirical data exist on the length of residence of non-nationals in general and the discrepancies between de facto long-term residence and possession of a permanent residence status in particular. However, it is plausible to assume that there are considerable discrepancies and that a significant proportion of de facto long-term residents are thus excluded from the protection conferred by denizenship and are left with a range of lesser statuses.[6]

The problem has hitherto hardly been taken up by governments, and regularisation programmes are on the whole only partial answers to the more fundamental problems posed by unequal access to rights.[7]

Finally, the debate over denizenship has a strong European bias.[8] The different paths taken by classic immigration countries, such as the US, Australia, New Zealand and Canada, where a permanent residence

> Comparative studies of the interlinkages between denizenship and
> citizenship in classic immigration countries on the one hand, and Europe,
> on the other, would be a promising topic for future research.

permit may be acquired at entry, suggests that the trend to denizenship as an alternative to citizenship for first generation migrants may be indeed a European peculiarity.[9] In the former, there seems to be also a strong expectation (and interest) that migrants admitted as permanent residents will eventually naturalise. As a corollary, citizenship is an instrument of migration policy and an essential element of the overall migration regime in these countries, whereas in Europe the link between citizenship regulations and the overall immigration regime has been far more tenuous. Much, however, depends on particular historical circumstances and thus may be subject to change.

The tendency in recent changes of immigration legislation in Europe to grant a secure residence status to highly skilled immigrants indicates a certain convergence with immigration practices in classic immigration countries.

Citizenship regulations in comparative perspective: Is there convergence?

As post-war labour migrants have turned into permanent immigrants, and, increasingly, citizens, the question as to how nation states organise access to, and loss of, citizenship has received considerable attention from a wide array of disciplinary angles and theoretical approaches. Douglas Klusmeyer (2001) notes in the introduction to a recent important study that 'citizenship has emerged as major thematic link connecting [a wide range of] policy domains', since it raises three fundamental issues: 'How the boundaries of membership within a polity and between polities should be defined; how the benefits and burdens of membership should be allocated; and how the identities of members should be comprehended and accommodated'. More than a decade after the publication of Rogers Brubaker's seminal study on citizenship policy in Germany and France (Brubaker 1992), both the sort of questions raised by Brubaker and the answers suggested by him and others have become increasingly complex. Brubaker put forward the hypothesis that citizenship regulations reflect different conceptions of nationhood. This idea has since been largely rejected and replaced by more nuanced interpretations of Brubaker's own case studies Germany and France. Moreover, the relationship between nation-state formation and the historical evolution of citizenship regulations has also been analysed in a number of other case studies (see Weil 2002 for France, Favell 1998 and Hansen 2000 for the UK, Gosewinkel 2001 and Preuss 2003 for Germany, Lefebvre 2003 for Belgium). In particular, Brubaker's underlying assumption that citizenship regulations show a certain internal consistency has been largely discarded. Instead, citizenship regulations are disentangled into various sets of rules each of which follows a slightly different logic: naturalisation rules for first generation migrants, access to citizenship for children born to parents with foreign citizenship, acquisition of citizenship through marriage, transmission of citizenship to children born to nationals abroad, and dual nationality (see Hansen & Weil 2001b). Some recent publications try to reassess Brubaker's long historical perspective of the evolution of citizenship in France and Germany (Weil 2002, Hansen 2000, Gosewinkel 2001). Most new comparative research focuses, however, on recent changes of citizenship as a result of mass migration and the convergence of citizenship rules across countries, in several important respects.

The remainder of this section is structured as follows: First, we will briefly reflect on the larger structural determinants of citizenship regulations, with a regional focus on Europe. In a second step, the debate on convergence or divergence will be reviewed, followed by a discussion of citizenship policies in 'non-western' countries of immigration. Finally, after discussing sending states' citizenship policies, empirical trends in regard to how states deal with the issue of dual citizenship will be sketched and reasons for recent policy changes explored.

The wider context: structural determinants of citizenship rules in 'wider Europe'

Recent debates over citizenship policy in Europe, both in the old Member States (EU-15) and on a European level, cannot be understood outside the specific context of large-scale and long-term immigration. The same is true for the evolution of citizenship policy in the post-war period in traditional immigration countries such as the US, Australia and Canada. Citizenship policy thus changed largely as a response to specific challenges posed by the presence of long-term migrants and their descendants and an overall concern for the integration of long-term resident non-nationals, even if there are significant deviations from this general pattern. There are some exceptions, such as Greek citizenship policy that largely addresses the issue of returning Greek migrants and that of ethnic Greeks from the former USSR, or German policy towards ethnic Germans from the same region. These concerns about external co-ethnic populations are also common in the new Member

States and candidate countries. Nevertheless, there is now a widely shared consensus that long-term migrants should, after a certain minimum period of residence, be given the opportunity to obtain the nationality of their country of residence, if they wish to do so. The consensus that there is a moral right for long-time residents of a particular country, to naturalise and that naturalisation should be seen as an important step towards full integration of migrants into the receiving society, has recently also been acknowledged by the Presidency Conclusions of the European Council at Tampere in October 1999 – a position endorsed by recent Commission policy statements.

But this view did not always prevail. Ethnic conceptions of nationhood formed citizenship policies of western countries until recently and continue to do so in many states, albeit in a modified way. Also, citizenship policies of western States were until World War II very much driven by overarching security concerns over the loyalty of non-citizens and ethnic minorities. Both ethnic minorities and aliens, including genuine refugees from persecution such as German Jews in wartime Britain, were thus often suspected of disloyalty and subjected to severe control.

However, the new geopolitical order that emerged after World War II as well as the establishment and consolidation of democracies in Western Europe and European integration facilitated the gradual desecuritisation of citizenship policy. Nevertheless immigration control and management continued to be dominated by security policy. In the field of migrant integration, massive labour migration led to gradual changes of conceptions of nationhood and the acceptance or even endorsement of the multicultural nature of most western post-war societies. This development called for a concomitant de-ethnicisation of citizenship (see Hansen & Weil 2001b, Joppke 2004). Particularly since 9/11 this liberal tendency has been replaced in many countries by a more restrictive integration policy focusing again on security issues.

By contrast, other countries such as the former communist countries in Eastern Europe or Turkey have quite different trajectories. There, labour immigration didn't occur until recently and even today only the more prosperous countries, such as the Czech Republic, Hungary and Slovenia, receive significant numbers of long-term international migrants, while in others, notably Poland, circulatory migration dominates. Still others, such as Turkey, Cyprus or the Baltic States, only serve as 'temporary' hosts for often undocumented transmigrants, ultimately bound to countries further west. The communist past of Eastern European states, and the authoritarian past of others (e.g. Cyprus and Turkey) meant that citizenship was devoid of most rights normally attached to it and, as a consequence, largely irrelevant as a policy area and as a 'political good' in the eyes of citizens. Similarly, the restrictions on exit often meant that emigrants, especially refugees lost any citizenship rights in their countries of origin once they migrated elsewhere, but especially to the west. At the same time the communist regimes, as well as Turkey, were heavily engaged in building nations based on the majority ethnic groups, even if some concessions were made to minority nation-building projects.

> The structural determinants of citizenship policies warrant further comparative study. In particular the question how conceptions of nationhood are related to citizenship policies is an unresolved issue and a promising field for future research.

The transition in the former communist countries to liberal democracies and its wider geopolitical ramifications initiated a major transformation of both majority and minority nation-building projects in Central and Eastern Europe and beyond. In this process, the issue of citizenship resurfaced in a number of ways. First, it was again posed in terms of security and loyalty (most prominently in the Baltic States; but also vis-à-vis autochthonous ethnic minorities with powerful kin-states as in Slovakia with respect to the Hungarian minority). Second, the issue of external minorities was raised again (in particular in Hungary towards the Hungarian minorities in Slovakia, Romania, and Serbia), sometimes also in terms of larger security concerns (e.g. in the case of Russia's largely unsuccessful attempts to act as an external protector of the Russian speaking minorities in the Baltic States). Similarly, citizenship in Cyprus is, in important regards, a security issue and touches a number of fundamental problems of the Cyprus conflict. How these issues (property rights, freedom of settlement, freedom of movement, the question of the Anatolian settlers etc.) will be resolved has important ramifications for an eventual settlement. Third, the new nation-building projects were extended to emigrant minorities and other dispersed co-ethnics with claims to citizenship of their kin-state or country of origin (Poland is an example both in regard to its emigrants to western countries and its diaspora in the former Soviet Union). Fourth, in successor states the formation of new nation states was often also seized as an opportunity to redraw the boundaries of the political community and to exclude particularly vulnerable or 'detested' groups from citizenship, either by law (as by the restoration of pre-Soviet nationality laws in the Baltics) or by other means.[10]

Thus, it seems plausible to assume that citizenship policies do indeed reflect wider historical experiences, such as migration or legacies of nation-building, but not necessarily in the way that Rogers Brubaker imagined.

The way that history impacts present citizenship policies is certainly worthy of much more comparative analysis. Also, one of the main arguments made in this section – that western states have desecuritised 'citizenship' and immigration policy, while in many other states security concerns are still rather important, is evidently subject to historical conjunctures. It may well be, that security concerns will again play a much more important role in citizenship policy of western states in the future.[11]

Access to, acquisition of and loss of nationality in liberal states – is there convergence or divergence?[12]

The comparative analysis of citizenship policies in a broad sense is not a completely new field of research. Pioneered by legal scholars (see notably the work of de Groot 1989), since the early 1990s the issue has increasingly also drawn the attention of social scientists. Not only the approaches taken by more recent studies but also the sort of questions asked are different from those posed by earlier works. What is perhaps more important, recent comparisons increasingly enquire to what extent citizenship policies across countries converge if certain similar structural conditions prevail (see Aleinikoff & Klusmeyer 2001, 2002; Hansen & Weil 2001a; Joppke 1999; Kondo 2001). In addition, citizenship regulations are no longer seen as comprehensive models but disentangled into various sets of rules (see above), allowing new perspectives on citizenship policies and a reformulation of the terms of the debate. Most importantly, it is increasingly recognised that the distinction between ius sanguinis countries on the one hand, and ius soli ones, on the other, may to some extent be a rather misleading dichotomy. There may be a few cases that seem to perfectly exemplify one of the two models. However, most states actually combine elements from both, for example, by providing for ius sanguinis transmission of citizenship for descendants of nationals born abroad, while applying ius soli to children of foreign residents born in the country.

In addition to the problematic interpretation of ius sanguinis and ius soli as 'models', the principles 'ius soli' or 'ius sanguinis' only describe transmission of citizenship from the first to second and later generations. Thus, acquisition of citizenship is never governed by these principles alone; citizenship can also be obtained by first generation migrants through naturalisation procedures, through marriage, by adoption, and other modes of acquisition.[13] Different features, therefore, determine access to citizenship (Eder & Giessen 2001; Kondo 2001; Weil 2001).

Historically, ius soli corresponded with the interest of traditional settler societies (e.g. the United States, Canada or Australia) to automatically confer citizenship to second generation immigrants in order to ensure their loyalty and to assert territorial sovereignty against immigrants' countries of origin.[14] The dominance of the ius soli principle in the UK, on the other hand, is a legacy of old and may be traced back to the 'common law doctrine of monarchical allegiance, which labelled as British subjects anyone perchance born within the king's dominions' (Everson 2003: 61). This principle prevailed in similar form in most pre-modern European societies until the Napoleonic wars.

Since World War II, European countries, such as the UK, which based their citizenship on this 'demotic'[15] principle experienced a rapid increase of 'new nationals' by sole fact of birth in the territory to an extent no longer acceptable to increasing proportions of the public. As a result, the UK gradually began to reverse its ancient tradition through the installation of a series of new immigration acts that put limits to the automatic access to British citizenship. This change of law was particularly directed towards the offspring of former colonial subjects who previously enjoyed direct access to British citizenship. Since the Nationality Act of 1981 ius soli is granted only to second generation immigrants born in the country if one parent has a permanent residence permit, whereas minors born abroad can acquire British citizenship only if they prove having lived in the UK for ten years without interruptions. Simultaneously, ius sanguinis transmission of citizenship for citizen's children born abroad was introduced. In 2004 automatic acquisition of citizenship at birth in the territory also came under attack in the Irish Republic where a plebiscite rendered a majority against unconditional ius soli.

Second-generation migrants

Despite becoming countries of immigration after World War II, many continental nation states retained ius sanguinis as the main principle governing the acquisition of citizenship by the second generation, leaving naturalisation as the main mode for acquiring citizenship by the greater part of the immigrant population. Moreover, in countries such as Switzerland, Germany and Austria, second and third generation migrants were considered foreign nationals and had access to nationality on the same terms as first generation migrants (Germany has radically changed its policy in 1999, while Austria introduced in 1998 merely a facilitated naturalisation procedure for children born to foreign nationals in the country). In Switzerland, a referendum in September

2004 overturned government plans to introduce facilitated naturalisation for the second and automatic ius soli for the third generation.

Many European states have recently introduced an entitlement or facilitated access to citizenship in order to promote the integration of second and third-generation immigrants. Thus, empirically, the trend in this particular dimension is towards convergence. Among Europe's states with a longer history of immigration, only Austria, Luxembourg and Switzerland remain as the 'odd men out'.

First-generation migrants

For those who arrive as first immigrants into the country, the most common way to acquire citizenship is through ordinary naturalisation procedures. To obtain the nationality of the country of residence, migrants usually have to meet a common set of requirements, namely a minimum residence period, no criminal record, sufficient financial means, and, increasingly, proof of 'integration', sometimes in the form of civics, language or wider 'assimilation' tests. Minimum residence requirements vary greatly between states. Even within a single country there may be considerable differences in the implementation of citizenship laws, in particular in federal states (see Bultmann 2002).[16] Most states allow for considerable administrative discretion, although an increasing number give an absolute right to naturalisation after a certain residence period, often differentiated for different categories of migrants. Certainly, much more research needs to be done on administrative practice and informal rules applied by regional or local authorities.

Among states that require a short minimum period of domicile are Belgium (3 years), Ireland (4), and Canada (4). In the middle range we find Denmark (9), Finland (6), France (5), the UK and the Netherlands (5), Sweden (5) and the United States (5). States with long residence requirements are Germany (8), Austria (10), Italy (10), Luxemburg (10), Portugal (10), Spain (10), Greece, (10) and Switzerland (12) (see table 1 in the annex as well as Gronendijk et al. 2000).

Recent reforms of citizenship legislation across Europe have seen a proliferation of 'integration' requirements. In other countries, for example the US, citizenship tests have a much longer tradition. In most states, though, 'integration' requirements are largely irrelevant in practice, as tests are simple and migrants resident for the required minimum period generally meet the specific conditions (language proficiency, minimum knowledge of the legal and political order). Thus, the obligation to prove 'sufficient' integration is deeply embedded in symbolical politics (Kostakopoulou 2003). Nevertheless, the recent reforms in the Netherlands, which introduced much stronger integration requirements in the form of a highly demanding assimilation and citizenship test, signal an important reversal of the general trend in citizenship policies in the past decades to gradually relax conditions for naturalisation and to move towards an understanding of citizenship as an entitlement for long-term first generation migrants. The Dutch reform had a massive and immediate impact on the numbers of naturalisations, as many applicants failed the tests. From the perspective of states, therefore, two opposing views on citizenship seem to emerge: one that sees citizenship as a means to integrate newcomers more fully into the national community and therefore welcomes the timely acquisition of citizenship, and a second, which sees citizenship as a 'prize', a reward and honour granted by the state on its own terms and by discretion.

Naturalisation by marriage, through adoption and by extension

Traditionally, foreign women could more or less automatically acquire citizenship by marrying a citizen husband. This automatism has been removed bit by bit in many countries since World War II, particularly since the 1980s (Sweden 1950, Denmark 1951, Portugal 1959, Italy 1981, Belgium and Greece 1984). Furthermore, the period until an application for the spouse could be submitted has been extended. These modifications were accompanied by a new concept: Men and women should be treated equally (mostly in the sense that from then on both had to apply for citizenship). Nevertheless, many states feared that marriages would be misused in order to get legal access to the territory. Therefore, specific residence and time limits were imposed before an application could be submitted. (Automatic) acquisition of nationality by adoption is very similar to obtaining citizenship by marriage. Yet, again, fearing potential abuse, states have increasingly restricted access to nationality for adopted children.

Research must take into account that access to citizenship is rarely a purely individual matter. Many migrants become citizens through marriage or extension of naturalisation to family members. Decisions about naturalisation are also often a family matter.

Finally, considerable numbers of non-nationals acquire citizenship by extension, that is, by virtue of an immediate family link to a primary applicant for regular naturalisation.[17] The conditions for the acquisition of nationality by extension (e.g. whether minimum residence periods are required or 'extraterritorial' naturalisations are allowed), and more importantly, changing state policies in this regard, have, however, received little attention so far.

State policies for admission to citizenship thus never target only the single migrant. For most people of migrant origin, access to citizenship is determined by their private relations of marriage or descent. The importance of these family contexts must also be considered when studying motives for naturalisation. Just as economic models of migration were for a long time based on oversimplified assumptions of individual rational choice and disregarded migrants' families as a relevant decision-making unit, so research on naturalisation must also consider how migrants' choices may be determined by family contexts.

Loss and renunciation of citizenship

While comparative legal studies on nationality laws generally include the conditions of loss and renunciation (see De Groot 2003 for an excellent recent comparative analysis), research on state policies towards migrants has always paid much more attention to citizenship acquisition by birth and naturalisation and often ignores whether and how a citizenship of origin is lost. Certain states (e.g. many Arab countries, see text box 2 below) still embrace the principle of 'perpetual allegiance' and do not permit any renunciation of citizenship whatsoever. In those states that do provide for loss of citizenship, conditions vary greatly. The acquisition of another nationality is probably the most frequent ground for the loss of citizenship but is difficult to implement as the rising incidence of dual nationality shows, even in those cases where both citizenship regulations involved theoretically require renunciation. Also, once renounced, a former citizenship may often be easily reacquired. The naturalising state generally has no information about such reacquisitions and can thus not enforce a legally prescribed withdrawal of its own citizenship.

> The loss of citizenship issue highlights the dual nature of citizenship as a domestic and international law instrument and the interdependency between national regulations.

Putting a focus on loss of nationality serves also as a useful reminder that citizenship has an important international dimension, not only in the sense that conflicts between states may arise that involve issues of citizenship (e.g. dual nationality and resulting conflicts of loyalty; or statelessness). Rules for access to citizenship for non-citizens as well as rules on loss of citizenship for current citizens also touch automatically on areas clearly outside a single state's jurisdiction. In other words, a state may seek to impose its own terms but can never be sure of another state's co-operation. States may want to avoid dual citizenship by requiring renunciation of a previously held nationality, but they cannot force the respective other state to release its citizens. Demanding renunciation of another state's citizenship of naturalising aliens is clearly within the naturalising state's powers and relatively simple to administer. Nevertheless, most liberal states now allow foreign nationals to keep their citizenship if renunciation is not possibly or comes at great cost. In case of their own citizens acquiring another citizenship, states that require renunciation have to rely on co-operation by the authorities of the other state. However, more and more sending states are deliberately giving up on such external renunciation requirements. Security concerns over the loyalty of citizens abroad have largely disappeared[18] and other possible disadvantages arising from citizens abroad acquiring another nationality are increasingly outweighed by the benefits of maintaining ties with a well-integrated expatriate community.[19]

At the same time, there seem to be increasing security concerns regarding states' 'domestic' citizenship policies, that is, citizenship rules for first and second-generation immigrants. Still, in some specific cases, notably the withdrawal of citizenship (e.g. in case the alien has obtained a states' citizenship fraudulently), the states' capacity to enforce their rules may be limited for the very same reasons that prevent them from controlling their own citizens' compliance with legal regulations when acquiring another citizenship abroad. In short, no state is obliged to take back former citizens.[20] In addition, international legal instruments preventing statelessness are arguably much stronger than those seeking to prevent dual nationality, at least in liberal states, since they are much more likely to be invoked by domestic courts. In several European states, however, fraudulent acquisition is regarded as such a compelling ground for withdrawal that even statelessness is accepted as a result.

Text Box 2: Gianluca Parolin, Citizenship and the Arab world

Dynamics of interaction between migration and citizenship in the Arab world are quite unique, as many factors interweave in the discourse. Unfortunately, this important group of countries has so far received little attention in research on citizenship.

Arab countries may be roughly divided into emigration and immigration countries, with a significant quota of inter-Arab migration. Gulf countries are traditionally receiving countries, while Mashreq and Maghreb countries are generally sending countries. Nonetheless, citizenship laws were inspired all over the Arab world by the same continental European model, and are based upon the same principles.

Stricter provisions for naturalisation and severe regulations for migrant labour, though, are found in Gulf legislations. All across the Arab world, from the Gulf to the Atlantic Ocean, two different sets of rules apply to Arabs and foreigners, raising the issue of a clear definition of who is to be considered an Arab. Naturalisation requirements are much fewer and lower for Arabs than for foreigners, but for both groups naturalisation is a very rare phenomenon in the Arab world, particularly in the Gulf. Conversion to Islam may be openly requested in the citizenship law – as it is in Kuwait – or rather be left to broad discretionary powers of the state.

When models are transplanted, some of their features quickly take root in the new context while others do not. A clear illustration of the former phenomenon is the idea of 'perpetual allegiance'. Ever since the Ottoman law, the state acknowledges a national's naturalisation in another country only if the individual had previously obtained special authorisation from the state, otherwise the state continues to consider such expatriates naturalised abroad as 'nationals'. The principle of perpetual allegiance still forms a major obstacle to renunciation of nationality and toleration of multiple nationality, it constrains the rights and duties of Arab expatriates, and provides justification for political control over migrants by their home countries.

In many Arab countries there are large sections of the population that have no citizenship status. Examining the historical and political regional context helps explain this phenomenon of statelessness. Generally the goal is to achieve a certain religious, sectarian, or ethnic balance between citizens and minority populations. But the denial of citizenship often causes tension in the social body, as recent events have shown throughout the region. A case in point is the status of Palestinians in other Middle East countries where they have taken refuge over the past fifty years. However, how are Palestinians considered when it comes to granting them naturalisation, and how many native populations have been denied citizenship? There is a lack of reliable data in this area and collecting them is difficult, since citizenship is a sensitive issue.

The flip side of the Janus-faced nature of citizenship (as both a domestically and internationally effective legal instrument) is that states may denaturalise citizens at their own will, with other states having little power to interfere with such a decision. In liberal states, deprivation of citizenship in individual cases on grounds of race, religion, ethnicity or 'subversive political activities' are arguably a thing of the past, but more authoritarian states often feel less bound by international agreements to reduce statelessness (see also the first section of chapter 3).[21]

Finally, large numbers of individuals and whole categories of persons were effectively deprived of nationality in the course of the breakup of the communist federations (Yugoslavia, Czechoslovakia, and the Soviet-Union), underlining the fact that loss of citizenship and statelessness remain pressing issues even today. However, while the Baltic States' citizenship policies towards the Russian minorities have received considerable attention from researchers and policy makers alike (see Barrington 2000, Brubaker 1994), no similar attention has been devoted to the equally challenging cases of Ex-Yugoslavia and the former Czechoslovakia.

Explaining citizenship policies in liberal states

The convergence of nationality laws in liberal states along a number of lines has been increasingly acknowledged and corroborated by a wide range of empirical evidence. However, are the factors leading to convergence the same or at least similar across countries? Are similar outcomes the result of a more or less uniform and unidirectional process of conscious policy decisions? Or are they rather the result of a complex mix of factors including wider processes of social change, transformations of legal traditions and conceptions of nationhood, and the nature of policy-making processes, which are specific to each country? Put in more general terms, what are forces driving citizenship policies? Which factors or set of factors influence the nature of citizenship laws? Do citizenship laws only define a privileged legal status and membership to the political community of the nation state or do they embody membership to the 'nation' as such, understood as an 'imagined community', a collectivity sharing a common past and destiny?

Several answers to these questions have been suggested in recent years, some more far-reaching (such as Rogers Brubaker's argument on the close interrelationship between citizenship policies and conceptions of nationhood) than others that advance more limited and specific explanations. Indeed, it seems plausible to assume that there are similar broader structural forces at work that help to explain the nature, scope and degree of politicisation of citizenship policy. Most importantly, citizenship policies in western liberal states cannot be understood outside the specific context of post-war mass-immigration.

In one of the major recent contributions to the comparative analysis of citizenship, Randall Hansen and Patrick Weil (2001b) take the argument a step further and argue that major changes of citizenship policy in liberal states typically occur in specific stages of a country's migration history. They develop three main hypotheses on the direction of policy changes: (1) While in periods of ongoing mass-migration access

> Research has refuted the assumption that citizenship policies are directly
> derived from ethnic vs. civic traditions of nationhood, but the complex
> relation between conceptions of national identity and citizenship remains
> an open question for comparative studies.

to citizenship is marked by restrictions and administrative discretion, (2) liberal states tend to liberalise naturalisation requirements when the immigrant population stabilises and has settled in the country for considerable time. However, (3) they also suggest that restrictions occur when citizenship policy becomes politicised and subject to party competition, as a result of which it is often reframed as an issue of national identity.

It is not by accident that Hansen's and Weil's hypotheses remain on a rather general and abstract level, pertaining only to the direction of policy changes but not to the general nature of policies or the specific form and content of acquisition and transmission rules. The latter still display considerable differences and idiosyncrasies, that may be explained only by recourse to broader historical processes at work, such as earlier citizenship laws and the historical context of their making, legal traditions, historical constellations of power, etc. Indeed, to a large degree citizenship policy making seems to be a showcase example of path dependence (Faist, Gerdes & Rieple 2004; Hansen 2002).

As Christian Joppke (2004) has recently shown, the way 'history' determines citizenship law is not necessarily straightforward. Often, the form and content of the law as well its preservation over time may be a mere 'accident', a result of a specific historical constellation that led to the crafting of the original law and, in regard to later periods, a result of the lack of consensus or constitutional limitations preventing the adoption of a new law. Alternatively, older citizenship regulations may be preserved simply because there are no incentives for policy makers to change the law and citizenship policy remains outside public debate. A good example is the origin of the ius sanguinis principle, adopted by virtually all European countries, except Britain, during the first half of the nineteenth century. The multinational Habsburg Empire, for example, adopted ius sanguinis as early as 1811. At that time, it was considered 'modern' and a break with the feudal ius soli tradition that made a subject of anyone born within the overlords' dominion. Ius sanguinis was retained as the guiding principle of citizenship legislation in virtually all successor states after the break-up of the empire. Britain's retention of the ius soli principle, on the other hand, is largely due to the fact that it had no formal citizenship law at all until 1948, when senior politicians could still deride the very notion of citizenship as 'republican' and alien to British tradition (Hansen 2002: 187). It is not difficult to see then that the application of a formal principle alone is a rather weak indicator of an 'ethnic' conception of nationhood. While it could still be argued that citizenship policies are influenced by the way the nation is conceptualised, it is misguided to assume that they simply reflect ethnic or republican conceptions of nationhood. In many cases, citizenship may be altogether decoupled from nationality, as could be argued in the case of the UK but also in multinational federal states such as Belgium or Canada. Thus, how citizenship relates to conceptions of nationhood must remain an open question.

> The role of epistemic communities and of imitation has been rather neglected in explaining similarities or convergence of citizenship policies across states.

There may also be other factors at work. David J. Galbreath has recently argued that 'epistemic communities' (legal scholars, lawyers, judges, officials drafting the legislation) have been a rather neglected issue and an underestimated factor influencing the nature and form of nationality laws (Galbreath 2004). As members of an epistemic community frame problems in a similar language, engage in scholarly discourses, thus learning from each other, and heavily draw on 'best practices' dear to their scholarly ethos, their influence in crafting legislation may be decisive, in particular when citizenship policy remains outside public debate and is left to specialised experts. Again, the case of the diffusion of the ius sanguinis principle across Europe in the first half of the nineteenth century may be a good example and a promising topic for comparative historical research.

There are however more immediate factors which determine the nature of citizenship policies and, particularly, the nature of changes of citizenship policy. A major possible factor, already pointed at in the preceding paragraph, concerns the arenas of policy making and the stakeholders involved. In most countries citizenship has become a controversial issue only fairly recently and up to then, was dealt with largely behind closed doors and by specialised experts. In that context, nationality laws may not attempt to attain specific goals other than the mere regulation of a legal status.

Party competition, particularly within wider debates on national identity and immigration, may eventually lead to a politicisation of citizenship policy and can thus influence the nature of policies adopted. These, however, may go in different directions – parties may seek to reach new groups of voters (e.g. among Hispanics in the US or Turks in Germany) and press for liberalisation of citizenship laws, or they may want to send symbolic messages to traditional client groups or the electorate in general, for example by arguing for assimilation tests or citizenship oaths (Kostakopoulou 2003).

There are several objectives policy makers may achieve through citizenship policy when the issue has become politicised.

a) Citizenship policy may be an instrument of immigration policy. The classic example is the UK where controlling post-colonial immigration to Britain was the major objective of the 1981 Nationality Act. But citizenship policies may also be changed in tandem with immigration policies. For example, access to citizenship may be facilitated as a concession towards immigrant minorities in return for more restrictive immigration policies, as was the case in Belgium in the early 1980s.

b) Citizenship policy may be conceived as integration policy: Integration has been a major issue in the recent German and Swedish reforms. Interestingly, in both cases, the integration argument was mainly raised to defend dual citizenship.

c) In sending states, citizenship policy is often a matter of 'diaspora politics'. It is driven by the desire to maintain links with a country's emigrants abroad, be it for economic, cultural or political reasons, as is arguably the case in Turkey and Mexico.

d) Citizenship policy may also be tied to more limited agendas, for example, in regard to social policy, especially in cases where welfare entitlements are linked to citizenship. In more general terms, citizenship may serve as an instrument to regulate access to scarce public goods (see chapter 1).

e) Finally, citizenship policy may serve an ultimate agenda of nation-building, as it currently does, for example, in the Baltic States.

Text Box 3: Tanja Wunderlich, Migrants' motivations to naturalise

The enactment of the 1999 Citizenship Law in Germany was preceded by an intense public debate on immigration, integration and the relationship between citizenship, national identity and belonging: Should naturalisation be regarded as an instrument of integration policy or should it be considered the 'crowning' of successful integration? In the case of dual citizenship, can people be loyal to two countries, and does naturalisation translate into a feeling of 'being German'? As in other countries, the controversy over the reform of citizenship legislation was largely based on normative arguments from the perspective of the receiving society, with little attention being paid to how migrants themselves perceive naturalisation. The latter was the focus of a recently completed research project at EFMS.*
Using qualitative interview methods and combining narrative inter-

view techniques with checklist-guided interview elements, twenty-six naturalised migrants from sixteen countries of origin were interviewed in Bamberg (Bavaria). The results suggest that migrants usually have multiple motives for applying for citizenship. Pragmatic motives, such as improvement of one's legal status and equal treatment, easier travelling and less 'red tape' were frequently cited by respondents. In addition, the acquisition of citizenship also reflected (a) feelings of belonging (applicants felt that they belonged to Germany rather than their country of origin), (b) motives related to the country of origin (e.g. avoidance of military service, no plans to return, feeling of insecurity when travelling with the old passport), (c) family-related motives (e.g. to ensure a better future for their children; a desire to have the same legal status as spouses). In terms of the decision-making process, two groups of applicants could be distinguished: (1) applicants who reached the decision very quickly as soon as they met the formal requirements and without much deliberation; and (2) applicants who took a long time to reach a decision whether to naturalise or not. Often, such persons were strongly involved emotionally, met resistance in their families, were afraid of the formal requirements, such as the language test, or simply did not want to give up their former nationality. Research results suggest that family, friends and social networks seem to play a decisive role in the decision to naturalise: By talking about their plans, applicants' families often became aware of what advantages the German passport might bring or faced the reality that they wouldn't return to their country of origin. In some cases this resulted in family chain-naturalisations. Also very important in the decision-making process are emotional aspects. Fear, doubts, feelings of betrayal to the home country and family play an important role in this process as do joy and relief after the administrative procedures have been completed. This was very vividly expressed when the interviewees described the situation when they finally received a German passport ('it was like Christmas'). The research also showed that while the majority of applicants had very positive experiences with German naturalisation officers, they often felt mistreated in the consulates of their countries of origin, which made the decision to give up their old nationality much easier. Asked about the consequences of naturalisation, interviewees felt that the possession of citizenship did – as expected – indeed ease their lives in a number of ways, most importantly, with regard to legal matters. In addition, interviewees felt that naturalisation

---

* European Forum for Migration Studies, 'Naturalisation and integration: the subjective dimensions of the change of citizenship', project carried out between October 2000 and March 2003.

had improved their chances to find jobs; furthermore, they felt more secure with German citizenship and protected when travelling abroad. Also, they reported that the right to vote linked to citizenship had increased their interest in politics. Very few interviewees, however, identified any impact in terms of their identity, cultural practices or intercultural social networks. The same holds true with respect to discrimination experiences. In conclusion, naturalisation seems to be fairly independent from 'integration', with no direct reciprocal link: persons already well integrated (e.g. second generation migrants), as well as others who make a conscious decision to spend their lives in Germany decide at some point to naturalise, mainly to make their lives easier. Only in respect of structural integration (labour market, political participation), can naturalisation indeed be a 'motor' for integration.

Citizenship in non-western countries of immigration

The study of citizenship has traditionally been limited to western countries of immigration. With dual citizenship emerging as one of the major issues in comparative analyses of citizenship, the importance of 'external citizenship' and (non-western) sending countries' policies towards their expatriates has been increasingly acknowledged. These policies impact not only on dual citizenship in western countries of immigration but also on the naturalisation behaviour of migrants more generally (see text box 3 above). Citizenship policies of non-western receiving states, however, have received little attention from mainstream migration research so far. As with regard to the status of foreigners more generally (see footnote 20), it seems that the general trend is that most developing countries in Asia, the Middle East and Africa are on the whole much more reluctant to grant membership rights to immigrants. Also, in lesser developed states, there is often a large gap between citizenship laws on the one hand and administrative practice on the other, perhaps more so in 'weaker' states and in federal polities. The often inconsistent and contradictory nature of citizenship laws contributes to this prevalence of discretion and unpredictability of decisions.[22] In addition, in many states the citizenship status of both citizens and migrants is often only poorly documented, if at all, leaving considerable room for political manipulation. For example, the exclusion of opposition politicians in sub-Saharan Countries from participating in elections or other political activities on grounds that they did not possess citizenship of the respective country or had acquired it fraudulently, has been a rather frequent phenomenon in recent years, with the case of former Zambian president Kenneth Kaunda being probably the best known example of this phenomenon. It is obvious that the nature of citizenship varies in different countries of the developing world. However, as their citizenship policies have been hardly studied many open questions remain. Developing countries are highly heterogeneous. Therefore a sensible first step for comparative analysis would be to look for groupings of countries with similar trajectories that could be reasonably studied together, such as the Arab world (see text box 2 above), sub-Saharan Africa (see Herbst 2000 for an analysis of citizenship regulations), Asian countries or Latin American states.

External citizenship policies of sending states

Issues relating to external citizenship of sending states – citizenship rights and obligations of persons residing outside their country of nationality, towards the latter (Brubaker 1989) – have been fruitfully explored in recent years, mainly in the context of the debate on dual nationality. While not necessarily limited to major sending states, external citizenship is arguably sociologically more relevant in their case. Specific citizenship policies towards nationals who reside abroad and their descendants are frequently adopted by states to maintain ties to their expatriates, whether or not they have acquired a foreign nationality and whether or not they follow a ius sanguinis or a ius soli tradition (see text box 4 below). Many sending states have also set up specialised administrative entities dealing with nationals, and sometimes former nationals, abroad. This is often an explicit acknowledgement of the valuable contributions citizens abroad make to the national economy (in the form of remittances) and to the state more generally,[23] but it is also motivated by efforts, in particular in more authoritarian states, to keep a certain level of control over emigrants. From the perspective of both migrants and the state, the maintenance of external citizenship ties may also reflect broader symbolic and cultural concerns. In some countries, notably the former communist states in Eastern Europe, a conscious effort is often made to re-establish links with relatively old migrant diasporas abroad, mainly by facilitating and encouraging the reacquisition of citizenship (see on Poland Górny, Grzymała-Kazłowska, Koryś & Weinar 2004).

Sending states' external citizenship policies are motivated by a mix of economic interests in remittances, of political interests in exercising control over expatriates and of cultural and symbolic nation-building policies.

In many states, citizens abroad are encouraged to retain their citizenship and transmit their nationality to their descendants, in others citizens may not be able to formally give up their nationality. Both policies contribute to the increasing incidence of dual nationality. External citizenship raises several issues: how citizenship policies of sending and receiving states interact with each other; which rights and duties are linked to external citizenship, e.g. whether certain rights and obligations often linked to domicile (e.g. voting and paying taxes) are extended to external citizens; why and how states encourage their citizens abroad to retain their nationality.

Text Box 4: Dilek Çinar, The politics of external citizenship – the case of Turkey

Turkey's growing interest in not losing its emigrants by way of naturalisation abroad manifested itself in an amendment of Turkish Citizenship Law in 1995. The amendment removed two major obstacles to naturalisation in countries that either accept dual citizenship merely under exceptional circumstances (Austria) or tolerate the emergence of dual citizenship only temporarily (Germany).* Since June 1995, Turkish emigrants who naturalise abroad can keep their citizenship rights in Turkey (apart from political rights). To this aim, a so-called 'pink card' has been introduced, which can be obtained by persons who have acquired Turkish citizenship by birth and who have been given permission by the Council of Ministers to be released from Turkish citizenship. The pink card provides former Turkish citizens with the rights to residence, employment, acquisition of real estate, inheritance, etc. (Dogan 2002: 127-130).** In addition, the amendment of 1995 abolished a provision according to which voluntary expatriation required compliance with military obligations. In other words, Turkish citizens of military service age can 'opt out' of Turkish citizenship in order to naturalise abroad without having first to serve in the Turkish army. Since then, naturalisations of Turkish citizens in Austria, and, particularly in Vienna, have been increasing significantly (Waldrauch & Çinar 2003: 276f).

Dual citizenship

As a reviewer of Hansen's and Weil's (2002a) and Martin's and Hailbronner's (2003) recent edited volumes on dual nationality critically remarks in response to a claim of the former book, the problem of dual nationality has, as nationality rules in general, repeatedly drawn the at-

---

* See Law No. 4112, 7 June 1995, on Amendments to the Turkish Citizenship Act (henceforth: Law No. 4112).
** See Article 2 of Law No. 4112.

tention of scholars of international law throughout the twentieth century and is thus not a particularly new issue (Donner 2004). Nevertheless, the issue has arguably remained somewhat marginal, both in public discourse and in wider academic debates, notably in the social sciences. From about the mid-1980s this has dramatically changed. Not only has academic interest in studying dual nationality considerably grown (Hammar 1985, Hansen & Weil 2001b), but debates on dual citizenship have also increasingly involved the wider public. For example, the issue of dual nationality was one of the most controversial issues in the 1999 reform of the German citizenship law, a showcase example of the politicisation of citizenship policy and probably the first time that dual nationality was such a high profile issue. Empirically, however, there are unmistakable signs of increased tolerance towards dual nationality (Hansen & Weil 2001b; Hansen & Weil 2002a), notwithstanding the fact that formal opposition to dual nationality has remained widespread.

While there are many studies of multiple nationality from an international law perspective, there is so far little research on structural conditions and political actors that have brought about the secular trend towards increasing toleration.

Traditionally, four reservations have been made in regard to the toleration of dual citizenship: the twin problems of multiple loyalty and related state security concerns; the possibility that dual citizenship may present an impediment to immigrant integration by encouraging attachment to a foreign country, its culture(s) and language(s); its potential as a source of conflicts over citizens' obligations (notably military service and taxation); and, finally, dual nationality as a source of inequality, since dual nationals may enjoy a range of rights and choices not available to singular nationals (Hansen & Weil 2002b: 7). A recent comparative study of Germany, the Netherlands and Sweden argues that liberal states ultimately face what the authors call a 'democratic proliferation' dilemma when adhering to the principle of avoiding dual nationality (Faist, Gerdes & Rieple 2004). If countries of origin don't provide for renunciation of citizenship or impose prohibitive costs on their citizens when they renounce their citizenship, liberal states are likely to grant exceptions by administrative fiat. The ex-post interpretation of these exceptions by courts and advocacy groups is likely to lead to an unintended expansive trend. However, even such an expansion on a case by case basis where dual nationality continues to be regarded as an exception rather than the rule need not eventually lead to formal toleration. Where renunciation is possible and relatively easy liberal states can still insist on enforcing it before awarding their nationality. This leads to a somewhat paradoxical constellation in which it is easier to become a dual national of a liberal democracy and an authoritarian state than of two states that share a commitment to democratic principles.

There is still relatively little work done on the conditions under which dual nationality is accepted and on the driving forces behind changes of citizenship policy. From the available evidence, however, it seems that the acceptance of dual nationality in Europe is very much an elite driven process, and involves immigrant groups if at all mainly as clients rather than as actors. Finally, there is little quantitative evidence on dual nationality. While the claim that the incidence of dual nationality is increasing is on the whole plausible, it is hard to prove empirically since states generally register only their own citizenship. Occasionally, multiple nationality is included in census or survey data, but reliable statistics would have to be international rather than national ones. If, as in the case of Turkey, sending states change their citizenship policies and make expatriation easier and less costly, it might also be expected that the incidence of dual nationality decreases. As empirical research on dual nationality is in its infancy, a large number of open questions remain. For example, virtually nothing is known on the incentives for and the motives of migrants to actively pursue the retention or reacquisition of their original citizenship.

Migrant choices, the impact of policies on naturalisation behaviour and the consequences of naturalisation

The final section of this chapter will deal with three closely interrelated issues: (1) migrant choices, their motives and the underlying causes for naturalisation decisions as well as incentives to naturalise; (2) the impact of policies on naturalisation behaviour, and (3) the consequences of naturalisation.

As most of the issues raised in this section are – to varying degrees – premised on the availability of quantitative data, the following discussion will devote special attention to statistical sources for research on naturalisation behaviour and the consequences of naturalisation. To be sure, migrants' motivation and naturalisation decisions may be usefully explored using qualitative approaches; similarly, the analysis of the impact of changing citizenship and immigration policies may also do without quantitative analysis, while an assessment of the consequences of naturalisation requires, as does the study of migrant choices, a mix of methods, depending on the nature of the issues studied.

In principle, four types of data on naturalisation can be distinguished[24]: (1) Administrative data on naturalisation (naturalisation statistics). In addition to total numbers of naturalisation, information on gender, age and former nationality are regularly available in most western countries. (2) A very robust source would be censuses, since they are among the most reliable data sources and are rich in information. However, censuses rarely contain information on naturalisation and naturalised persons.[25] In some countries, censuses (e.g. the US) provide indirect information on acquisition of citizenship allowing for cross-tabulations of country of birth, citizenship and country of birth of the parents from which numbers of naturalised first generation migrants can be derived. (3) Population registers, for example in Norway and Belgium, may contain information on naturalised persons. Sometimes (e.g. in the Nordic countries) population registers can be linked to a variety of other data sets containing, for example, socio-economic indicators and are thus particularly useful for studies of the consequences of naturalisation or possible processes of self-selection. (4) In some cases surveys may provide excellent additional information on topics often not covered by official statistics, such as the intention of migrants to naturalise, expectations tied to the acquisition of citizenship, and dual nationality (see Council of Europe 1995, Eurostat 2002).[26]

The most obvious data sources are naturalisation figures, which, by themselves, however, provide only limited information. Naturalisation rates are a more important indicator of changing migrant choices and changing contextual factors (mainly sending and receiving states' citizenship policies) of migrant naturalisation decisions.[27] Naturalisation rates – the ratio of naturalisations in a given year to the foreign population at the beginning of the year[28] – have been frequently used in arguments on the degree of 'restrictiveness' or liberality of citizenship laws, and, by extension, of immigration regimes more generally. Sometimes, they are also interpreted as indicators for the legal integration of migrants (see Council of Europe, 1995). Naturalisation rates, however, are in fact rather crude indicators. Most obviously, they do not measure how many among immigrants eligible to naturalise decide to do so, since the denominator includes the whole resident population of foreign nationality rather than only those who meet residence and other conditions for applying. Naturalisation rates are therefore importantly influenced by migration inflows that have nothing to do with either the rules for admission to citizenship or the propensity of an immigrant cohort to naturalise. This propensity may be influenced by a variety of factors, including demographic, political and economic ones. The interpretation of naturalisation rates therefore requires detailed knowledge about these contextual factors and, ideally, additional statistical data. Moreover, official migration statistics often cover a limited range of characteristics, for example, the legal grounds for acquisition of nationality (e.g. marriage, ordinary naturalisation, facilitated acquisition, re-acquisition etc.) are often not included. Specific modes of acquisition (e.g. by marriage or adoption) may not be covered at all by naturalisation statistics. Automatic acquisition by birth is never included in these statistics. The difference between ius soli and ius sanguinis regimes is, however, crucial when comparing naturalisation rates across countries, since native-born second generations are counted among the foreign population in the latter.

A range of issues – most importantly socio-demographic characteristics of immigrant groups, their motivations to naturalise, their future plans, etc. requires additional data not easily available in most European countries. Thus, for European countries as a whole, there are only a very limited number of studies that analyse the relationship between immigrants' characteristics and their naturalisation behaviour in more detail (see for example Diehl & Blohm 2003).

> Studies of migrants' motives for naturalisation should highlight the interplay between immigrant and citizenship policies on the one hand, and migrant choices on the other.

Three sets of factors can be distinguished that influence naturalisations: those that have to do with the country of residence; those that relate to the country of (former) citizenship; and, finally, characteristics of migrants (migrant groups) eligible for naturalisation. With respect to factors relating to the 'receiving' society, immigration and citizenship policies are probably the most important ones. Changes of citizenship laws, notably restrictions on access to nationality, may encourage migrants to naturalise before the new policy takes effect, thus leading to brief but significant increases in naturalisations, as was the case in the UK in the mid-1980s. Most importantly, certain conditions or the costs involved in obtaining nationality may deter naturalisations. This seems to be true for the recently introduced citizenship tests in the Netherlands. Similarly, it is plausible to assume a direct relationship between immigration policy and naturalisation behaviour: the more precarious the status of foreign residents, the more attractive is citizenship for foreign residents (see also text box 3 above). Thus, restrictive changes in laws regulating family reunification and denizenship may lead to an upsurge in naturalisations, while the reverse – an improvement of the legal status of foreign nationals may cause a decrease in the naturalisation propensity of migrants.[29]

With respect to the country of origin, a variety of factors are important, among them citizenship policies of sending states (whether it is easily possible to renounce citizenship and which costs are incurred when doing so, e.g. loss of inheritance rights or administrative fees), the political and economic situation in the country of origin, and the right to return. None of these has easily foreseeable consequences. On the contrary, they may entail the opposing decisions either to retain the original nationality or to acquire a (western) citizenship.[30]

Finally, characteristics of migrants themselves are an important factor influencing their naturalisation propensity and, consequently, naturalisation rates. Among the factors that may be important are immigration history, i.e. the time of migrants' arrival in their country of residence; socio-demographic characteristics such as sex, age, occupational status and place of birth (in country or abroad); migrants' future migration plans; knowledge about options to naturalise; the presence of emotional, social or family ties to the country of residence and country of origin (see Diehl & Blohm 2003); a desire for political participation in the country of residence that depends strongly on the political opportunity structure; and the influence of ethnic networks and elites on migrants' political choices.

> Surprisingly little is known about the consequences of naturalisation, both in economic and in political regards.

An emerging issue of research, little studied so far in Europe, but with important pioneering studies in the US and Canada, is the question whether the acquisition of citizenship has a positive impact on the naturalised person's socio-economic integration. In Europe, detailed datasets (with longitudinal data) that permit an in-depth analysis of socio-economic consequences of naturalisation matching research done in the US and Canada are available only in Scandinavia, the Netherlands and in Belgium.[31] One of the main issues in regard to the consequences of naturalisation is whether or not processes of self-selection are at work, that is, whether socio-economic (and perhaps also cultural) integration impacts positively on the naturalisation propensity of migrants rather than being a consequence of naturalisation (see text box 5 below).

Qualitative data, on the other hand, suggest that migrants often feel that their opportunities in the labour market, and thus their socio-economic integration has indeed improved with naturalisation. There is also some evidence (for example in the French *Histoire de Vie*-Survey) supported also by studies in the US that citizenship has noticeable positive effects on 'soft' indicators of socio-economic integration, for example on employment conditions and labour relations, without necessarily leading to rising wages or change of occupational status (the most common indicators used to assess socio-economic integration). Thus, the possession of citizenship may allow migrants to change employers more readily or to engage in trade unions. The question whether or not socio-cultural characteristics (a sense of belonging, social networks etc.) are important for naturalisation decisions has been studied only to a limited extent (but see Diehl & Blohm 2003). Finally, to what extent citizenship impacts on political views, migrants' interest in politics and political participation is a question difficult to answer (see for some evidence on this issue text box 3 above). As Bousetta and Martiniello (2003) have shown, the acquisition of citizenship may also encourage political participation of migrants in their countries of origin rather than only or predominantly in the country of residence.

Text Box 5: Jean-Louis Rallu, Naturalisation, a factor of economic integration?

Naturalisation grants immigrants the same rights as citizens and is therefore a central piece of socio-political integration. Is it the same for socio-economic integration? Cross-sectional census data show that naturalised people have higher qualification, occupation and income than foreigners. However, there is a need to disentangle effects of naturalisation itself from effects of self-selection, i.e. factors that make upwardly mobile immigrants more likely to naturalise.

According to the French 'Histoire de Vie' survey, migrants who naturalise improve their work situation well before naturalisation, and even more before than after for males. So, this is clearly a selection effect (Rallu 2004). However, seeking to naturalise also pushes migrants to improve their language ability and invest in human capital. Moreover, naturalisation gives access to public sector jobs, makes it easier to quit an employer voluntarily to look for better wages, and to enrol in trade unions. French data show smaller proportions of time spent as unemployed after naturalisation than before. An American study (Bratsberg, Ragan & Nasir 2002) proves that wages increase more after naturalisation than before, showing that more benefits are attached to citizenship itself than to investment for naturalisation. A shift to white-collar jobs occurs immediately after naturalisation, but access to public sector or union jobs and wage increases occur gradually over the period following naturalisation. Different results in French and US data may be linked to higher socio-economic status reached by immigrants in America.

US census data also show that people with highest qualifications, occupations and incomes are less frequently naturalised than those in a medium situation. High human capital enables people to make their way without naturalising. Similar results emerge from a recent

> Canadian study that shows high naturalisation rates for Chinese and Indian origin immigrants but low for European and US-American ones (Devoretz & Pivnenko 2004). Naturalisation is a factor of economic integration, but integration remains easier for those who have high qualification.

Perspectives for research

Traditionally, the analysis of the legal status of foreigners and migrants' transition to full citizenship has been studied in a legal or normative perspective. While these approaches remain important, they need to be complemented by others that will make it possible to make statements about the practical consequences of various regulations or the reasons for the adoption of particular rules. Nevertheless, there is a broad range of legal issues deserving more attention, for example, what rights 'denizenship' represents, how access to this status is regulated, or to what extent immigration laws and other relevant legislation (e.g. aliens employment laws) live up to anti-discrimination standards in liberal democratic states. The linkages and the relationships between immigrant policy and citizenship policy could be fruitfully explored to answer a series of questions regarding, for example, the nature of denizenship (whether it is indeed an alternative to citizenship or rather, as in classic immigration countries, a transitory status or a concession to certain groups of 'desired' migrants) or about the interplay between migration and citizenship policy reforms. In regard to both citizenship policy and the regulation of the statuses of foreign migrants, historical research could provide important insights into long-term trajectories and structural determinants of a contemporary policy.

Much more attention needs to be devoted to the study of administrative practice. Finally, empirical research on the consequences of a given legal status for individual migrants in social, economic and political respects and migrants' responses and choices under the particular constraints of a given status is rarely carried out, though crucial for evaluating policies and providing recommendations.

3 EU citizenship and the status of third country nationals

Bernhard Perchinig

The roots of Union citizenship

The roots of Union citizenship can be traced back to the 1970s when Community politicians first began to discuss 'European identity'. Initial concepts merely included student mobility, exchange of teachers and harmonisation of diplomas. A broader approach emerged at the 1973 Copenhagen summit where the European Commission suggested the introduction of a 'passport union' as well as 'special rights' for citizens of Member States (Wiener 1997: 539). These were defined as the 'political rights traditionally withheld from foreigners[1]': the right to vote, the right to stand for election and the right to hold public office. Member States were to grant these rights, which were, and in general still are, tied to naturalisation, to resident citizens of another Member State (Wiener 1997: 540). Until then mobile Community workers had only benefited from labour-related rights. Hence, migration to another Member State meant disenfranchisement. In 1975 the Heads of Government of Belgium and Italy for the first time proposed to enfranchise all Community nationals on the local level (Connolly, Day & Shaw 2005: 6). The Commission's technical report on special rights even went further by stating that these 'first and foremost' imply 'the rights to vote, to stand for election and to become a public official at local, regional and national levels' (Connolly, Day & Shaw 2005: 8). Although the report is not completely clear on this subject, the formulation 'at local, regional and national levels' suggests that Community citizenship was meant to include not only local but also regional and national suffrage.

In the 1980s, the prevailing political paradigm changed towards privileging 'negative integration'. This renewed focus on economic integration and the rights associated with freedom of movement pushed political participation into the background of debates on European Union citizenship. As a consequence, the sole steps towards reaching this goal in the 1980s were three directives establishing the right of residence for workers and their families as well as for students and the 'Social Charter' introducing social rights for Community citizens (Wiener 1997: 542). These improvements of social and economic rights for Community citizens residing in another Member State were, however, not accompanied by any political rights. Whereas Community workers were granted economic and social rights in the 'Community Charter of Fundamental Rights for Workers' in 1989, European citizenship practice did not include any political rights before 1992 when the Treaty of Maastricht was signed. Only then citizenship was defined as one of the three pillars of European political union. The provisions on citizenship, which were inserted into Article 8–8e (now 17–22) of the EC-Treaty, conferred the right to vote and stand for elections in municipal and in European elections in the Member State of residence to all citizens of a Member State, and not only to workers, as had been suggested by the Danish government (Connolly, Day & Shaw 2005: 12).

It is interesting to note that in the debate the European Parliament emphasised the need to rethink the 'traditional dichotomy between citizen and foreigner' (European Parliament 150/34 final: 9, cited in Wiener 1997: 547). To overcome this dichotomy, the Parliament and relevant NGOs demanded the extension of Union citizenship to 'every person residing within the territory of the European Union' (ARNE-Group 1995, cited in Wiener 1997: 547). This demand marks a significant turn from national to residence-oriented citizenship which has, however, not been put into practice. For, although the extension of the local franchise to Union citizens reflected a shift of the focus of belonging from the state to the place of residence, third country nationals were excluded from this development. In this respect Union citizenship remained tied to the nation-state framework, which it otherwise intended to transcend.

The effect of Union citizenship on the discourse about the integration of third country nationals on the European and the Member State levels has not been studied thoroughly and deserves further attention.

In effect Union citizenship instituted a new type of fragmented citizenship: Union citizens possess civil, social and political rights (and duties) with regard to the nation state whose nationality they hold; they enjoy residential and social, but not the full range of political rights vis-à-vis a second Member State in which they reside. Political rights are only granted at the local and the European levels but not at the politically more relevant nation-state level. Furthermore, rights of Union citizenship, particularly the right of residence, may still be revoked in case of threat to public order. Third country nationals enjoy social rights, providing that they are members of the labour force, but no other rights comparable to those of Union citizens (except for third country family members of Union citizens residing in another Member

State) and no political rights at all. Thus the current form of Union citizenship, although extending the rights of Union citizens in other Member States, has not overcome the boundaries of state-based nationality. On the contrary, it has cemented the clear divide between nationals, Union citizens from another Member State and third country nationals.

Whereas the strategies of political actors involved in the making of European migration policies have to some extent been studied (Favell 2001, Geddes & Guiraudon 2002, Guiraudon 2001, 2003), research on the politics of European citizenship policy is still quite limited. This research gap contributes to the low level of visibility of the issue in the public discourse on European integration. In particular, too little attention has been devoted to the role of the European Court of Justice (ECJ) in the development of Union citizenship practice. In this respect, the case of Rudy Grzelczyk[2] deserves specific attention. This case concerned the access of a French national studying in Belgium to social benefits. Having first received these, Mr. Grzelczyk was declined the payment on grounds that he was a national of another Member State and never had been a member of the labour force in Belgium. Mr. Grzelczyk appealed to the ECJ that decided in his favour. This decision includes the institution's most focused statement on Union citizenship so far, stating that 'Union citizenship is destined to be the fundamental status of nationals of the Member States, enabling those who find themselves in the same situation to enjoy the same treatment in law irrespective of their nationality, subject to such exceptions as expressly provided for.' Although the case concerns a Union citizen living in another Member State, this statement of the Court clearly extends the idea of non-discrimination far beyond the realm of labour-related rights. The explicit formulation seems to indicate that it intends to attribute a new importance to Union citizenship, which, nevertheless, still works like a glove turned inside out: 'It cannot act within the territory of nationality but only outside it though it purports to express citizen rights" (Guild 2004: 14).

European Union citizenship practice is an underresearched issue. The low participation of migrant Union citizens in local and European elections derserves further examination, as it might demonstrate the limited capacity for integration of the current model of Union citizenship.

The development of Union citizenship may be understood in a Marshallian tradition as a dynamic process driven by the tension between market-oriented and political rights, which, in effect, has led to a gradual extension of political rights for Union citizens (Guild 2004). The lack of political rights of mobile Community workers had become salient and the distinction between nationals and Member State citizens had lost its legitimacy only after – based on the idea of market equality – economic and social rights of nationals and Union citizens living in the same Member State had been approximated. Political rights at the local and European level were thus eventually granted to mobile Community citizens also in order to further promote such mobility. Since Maastricht, this dynamic seems to have come to a halt. Neither the Charter of Fundamental Rights nor the Draft Constitutional Treaty include a further reform of voting rights. It is presently an open question whether the concept of European citizenship will ever be further developed towards a federal model, which would have to include voting rights in the constitutive units of the federation, i.e. the Member States.

As no reporting procedure has been implemented, there is no comprehensive information available on the transnational voting practices of Union citizens. With regard to elections to the European Parliament, the available data show a significantly lower turnout of Union citizens living in a Member State whose nationality they do not hold as compared to nationals of that state. Not only registration in voting registers is low. With the exception of the Irish Republic (turnout-rate 1999: 43,89 per cent), turnout-rates in 1999 in most Member States have been lower than 30 per cent, and in six Member States lower than 10 per cent (Connolly, Day & Shaw 2005: 16). There are no data available on turnout rates for municipal elections, but the low number of non-nationals elected to municipal councils reported to the Commission clearly shows that Union citizens are not well represented in local councils (Connolly, Day & Shaw 2005: 16) and that they do not often make use of the political opportunity structure available to them.

Union citizenship or European denizenship?

From a theoretical point of view, the concept of Union citizenship poses several questions. First and foremost, the body politic to which Union citizenship refers – the European Union – is not the body conferring or withdrawing the status. Union citizenship is conceptualised as a supplement to nationality of a Member State, thus its acquisition or loss is regulated by rules outside the legislative procedures of the European Union (Preuss, Everson, Koenig-Archibugi & Lefebvre 2003: 5). The ECJ has stated in the Michelletti case[3] that the national competence of a Member State to recognize a person as a national of another Member State must be exercised with due respect for Community law.

This also might be interpreted to imply that acquisition and loss of citizenship must be exercised with the same due respect. However, this judgement has not had a major impact (cf. Guild 1996: 45, de Groot 2003: 19). Thus granting and withdrawing Union citizenship remains the sole competence of the Member States, which – according to their national traditions of citizenship – employ dramatically different legal regulations and practices[4].

> Member States are the gatekeepers for access to Union citizenship. Their divergent policies of citizenship acquisition at birth and by naturalisation impact on the political and social integration and mobility of immigrants in Europe.

There is some evidence of convergence with regard to access for second generation immigrants and a trend towards liberalisation in most Member States. However, nationality laws in the Member States stay divergent with regard to most other aspects, e.g. the implementation of ius soli, waiting periods or the extension of citizenship to family members (cf. Hansen & Weil 2001b: 11ff.). In effect, the boundary between citizens and non-citizens varies depending on country of residence and citizenship policies in that country: Third country nationals will acquire the right to naturalise in one Member State after three to five years and may then take up residence in another Member State, while others with similar migration biographies who have settled in this latter state might still face a threat of expulsion due to minor offences. As long as each Member State continues to hold the sole right to regulate acquisition and loss of citizenship, Member States can even undermine Union policies with regard to the integration of immigrants by setting strict standards for naturalisation or enhancing the differences between the legal position of third country nationals and their own nationals. Thus Union citizenship as 'citizenship of attribution' (Wihtol de Wenden 1999: 95) has not contributed to the equalisation of the status of third country nationals in the territory of the European Union.

> On a theoretical level, the adequacy of the term 'citizenship' for the status of Union citizens residing in another Member State and its potential for development, particularly with regard to political integration in that Member State, have to be examined more thoroughly.

Until 2004 Union citizens enjoyed strong protection only in the areas of labour market participation, access to social rights, and antidiscrimi-

> Research has refuted the assumption that citizenship policies are directly derived from ethnic vs. civic traditions of nationhood, but the complex relation between conceptions of national identity and citizenship remains an open question for comparative studies.

nation. Since 2004 their right to residence has been strengthened considerably.[5] From a theoretical point of view, the use of the term 'citizenship' for the status of Union citizens is nevertheless still questionable. Measured against an understanding of citizenship as a bundle of rights securing civil, social and political participation, the rights conferred to Union citizens outside the state of their nationality fulfil these criteria only in the field of social rights and security of residence. Access to political rights and higher public offices still is limited. The content of European citizenship has therefore been described as anaemic (Follesdal 2001: 314) and as characterized by a 'striking absence of rights that could trigger a more active concept of citizenship' (Prentoulis 2001: 198, cited by Preuss et al. 2003: 5). This lack of active citizenship raises the question whether Union citizenship ever will develop integrative powers comparable to those of Member State citizenship.

In an optimistic view, Union citizenship might be understood as an 'aspirational citizenship' with a potential for continuous further development. The current implementation of antidiscrimination provisions into the EC-Treaty and the Charter of Fundamental Rights may be seen as an example of the developmental potential of the concept. Nevertheless, both reforms do not improve the political opportunity structure for Union citizens. This issue is closely related to the institutional structure and the democratic deficit of the European Union. As long as the Council, and not the European Parliament, is the main decision-making body, the rights to vote and stand as a candidate for the European Parliament are no adequate substitutes for the right to vote in elections for national parliaments since these are the only institutions controlling the heads of government and ministers who forge the decisions of the Council.

European citizenship and policies vis-à-vis third country nationals

Up to the 1990s, the connection between European polices vis-à-vis third country nationals and Union citizenship was rather weak. Until the 1992 Maastricht Treaty, immigration policies were developed in extra-European fora mainly concerned with security issues (Trevi-group,

Ad-hoc-group immigration, Schengen group etc.), whereas policies vis-à-vis third country nationals (often also termed 'integration policies') were dealt with in the framework of social and regional policy and, because of jurisdiction of the ECJ on the EEC-Turkey Association Agreement, in the Association Council.

It took the Commission until 1985 to publish a suggestion for a Decision of the EC to consult with non-Member-States on immigration policy. This development prompted some Member States to approach the ECJ on the question of the Commission's competence to deal with migration policy which it based on its competence in the field of social policy, determined in Art. 118 European Community Treaty (TEC).

The ECJ confirmed this competence but denied it in the field of culture.[6] Nevertheless, this decision opened the door to a host of legal and funding measures for the integration of immigrants into the labour market and society. From the mid 1980s onwards, measures for the integration of immigrants became an important element within general labour market programmes funded by the European Social Fund (ESF), such as 'Employment', 'Integra' or 'Adapt'; and at the beginning of the 1990s the Commission also started to fund measures against discrimination. Since the mid 1990s the integration of immigrants also became an important element in programmes of the Regional Funds, e.g. 'URBAN' or 'INTERREG'. Furthermore, the European Commission pressed in 1997 for an amendment of Regulation (EC) 1408/71 *on the application of social security schemes to employed persons and their families moving within the Community in order to give* third country nationals access to social rights. This was eventually realised in Regulation (EC) 859/2003.

> The important role of the Association Agreement with Turkey for the development of EU migration policy illustrates that policy outcomes depend not only on explicit policy making in the Council, Commission and Parliament but also on the – often unintended – effects of ECJ decisions.

In the mid 1980s the Association Agreements with third countries, particularly the EEC-Turkey Association Agreement and the Decisions of the Association Council 2/76, 1/80 and 3/80[7], became relevant for EC migration policy making. The Agreement was concluded in 1963 and envisaged a gradual establishment of closer economic links with Turkey with a view towards eventual membership. It included provisions on the progressive introduction of freedom of movement for workers (Art. 12), establishment (Art. 13) and services (Art. 14). In 1970 an Additional Protocol was negotiated, setting a timetable for i.a. the gradual establishment of freedom of movement for Turkish workers to be implemented between 1 December 1976 and 30 November 1986 (Cicekli 2004: 2). However, this goal conflicted with the immigration policies of the Member States which had introduced restrictions on immigration in the 1970s. In this situation the ECJ became the main actor. In a series of 24 decisions between 1987 and 2004 (Cicekli 2004: 3), the Court established a wide-ranging interpretation of the decisions of the Association Council 1/80 and 3/80 whose effect was to approximate the right of Turkish members of the workforce and their families to the rights of Community workers, including the prevention of expulsion on general preventive grounds.[8] The ECJ also applied a broad concept of family, including the stepson of a Turkish migrant worker in the definition of a family member.[9] On the other hand, Turkish workers who were no longer part of the workforce were excluded from the protection of the Agreement and the Association Council decisions (Cicekli 2004).[10] Thus the ECJ has established a clear demarcation line between rights associated with labour-market participation and the extension of rights to non-members of the labour market that has occurred in the field of European citizenship policies. This highlights the limits set by the labour-market orientation of the Association Agreements.

In the area of traditional EU policy making migration issues were moved closer to the European institutions in the Treaty of Maastricht that defined immigration as an 'issue of common interest' and absorbed the previously existing fora into the so-called 'Third Pillar'. Although this pillar mixed intergovernmentalism with elements of the Community method in a complicated and cumbersome decision-making process, its results were limited to security concerns. The deficiencies of the 'diluted intergovernmentalism' (Kostakopoulou 2000:498) of Maastricht led the Council and the Commission to agree on the need to bring migration policy under Community competence, which eventually was agreed in the 1998 Treaty of Amsterdam.

This latter treaty did not only set up a new institutional framework including the majority of former third-pillar issues under Community competence, it also extended this competence into areas of immigrant integration. This transfer was to be completed within five years after its entry into force (i.e. by 1 May 2004). However, the Tampere European Council of 1999 prematurely transferred the right of initiative to the European Commission and thus strengthened the position of the latter considerably (cf. Apap & Carrera 2003: 2-4, Benedikt 2004: 63-143, Kraler, Jandl & Hofmann 2006, Schibel 2004).

The refugee crisis in Kosovo and the lack of coherent Union policies in the field provided the background for this meeting devoted to Justice and Home Affairs issues. The conclusions of this summit clearly sketched the approximation of the legal status of long-term residents with that of Union citizens as a major goal for a future EU immigration policy: 'The legal status of third country nationals should be approximated to that of Member State nationals. A person, who, having resided legally in a Member State for a period of time still to be determined, and who holds a long-term residence permit, should be granted a set of uniform rights in that Member State which are as near as possible to those enjoyed by EU citizens; e.g. the right to reside, receive education, and work as an employee or self-employed person, as well as the principle of non-discrimination vis-à-vis the citizens of the State of residence. The European Council endorses the objective that long-term legally resident third country nationals be offered the opportunity to obtain the nationality of the Member State in which they are resident' (Presidency Conclusion 1999: 21). In the following years, references to the Tampere conclusions were implemented into i.a. the European Employment Strategy and the Lisbon strategy.

> The aspirational programme for a migration policy of the European Union set up in Tampere has not been accomplished so far. This opens the question under which conditions European Union migration policy endeavours are likely to succeed or destined to fail.

In its Communication on a Community immigration policy, already presented in November 2000, the Commission sketched the outlines of a Union immigration and integration policy shaped by the 'spirit of Tampere'. The Communication confirmed the need for developing a common EU policy concerning 'separate but closely related issues of asylum and migration' (COM 2000 (757) final: 3). Acknowledging the demographic need for immigration, the paper demanded the opening of legal channels of immigration for labour migrants (COM (2000) 757 final: 3) and the development of a common policy for controlled admission of economic migrants. With regard to the legal status of third country immigrants, the Communication suggested a wide-ranging approximation of their legal status with those of nationals of the Member States, coining the term 'civic citizenship' for the ideas elaborated in the Tampere Presidency Conclusions. The contours of this new concept and its potential implications will be discussed in a separate section below.

In the area of 'hard law', the 'spirit of Tampere' was far less successful. Between 1999 and 2001, the Commission published several proposals for Council Directives regulating the status of third country nationals, i.a. with regard to the right to family reunification, the status of long-term residents and entry for paid or self employment.[11] These proposals were driven by the idea of approximating the rights of third country nationals with those of Union citizens as far as possible in the respective fields.

In the consecutive negotiations in the Council the directives both on family reunification and on the status of long term residents were watered down considerably (cf. Apap &Carrera 2003). After substantial pressure from the old 'guest-worker states' Austria and Germany in particular, the directive on entry for employment failed altogether.

The other two directives were agreed in the Council in 2003.[12] Particularly the directive on long-term residents gives Member States rather broad discretion, making it likely that major provisions will be implemented by political actors only after decisions of the ECJ. With regard to the family reunification directive, the European Parliament already has approached the ECJ, arguing that the limitations on family reunification laid down in the directive might violate the European Convention on Human Rights. Although the directives improve the status of third country nationals in some areas, such as social rights, family reunification and freedom of movement, their rights are still limited compared to those of Union citizens (see also text box 6 below). For example, only migrants residing in a Member State for more than five years may profit from the long-term-resident directive. Both directives do not guarantee in any way a homogeneous status of third country nationals throughout the European Union. Bilateral agreements with third countries and all more favourable provisions of the Association and Cooperation Agreements may be retained (Apap & Carrera 2003: 21). Furthermore, the directives contain several serious limitations of the rights conferred to long term residents when these appear to conflict with public policy goals and public security.

Union citizenship still is a highly hierarchical 'citizenship of reciprocity'. 'At the centre we find the nationals of the each State living in their own State, then the Europeans whose rights are reciprocal to those given to foreigners[13] in other European states, then the long term non-European residents, the non-European non-residents, the refugees, and at the margins, the asylum seekers and the illegals' (de Wenden 1999: 96). Although the 2003 Directive on Long Term Residents[14] transfers some of the rights of Union citizens to this group of third country nationals, their status still cannot be compared with that of Union citizens. Politically, the debate on Union citizenship with its focus on Member State nationals has seriously undermined the idea of a 'citizenship of residence' for which migrants' organisations mobilized in the 1970s and 1980s (de Wenden 1999: 96). It resurfaced only in 2000 with the introduction of the concept of 'civic citizenship' in the Commission's Communication on a Community Immigration and Integration Policy (COM (2000) 757 final).

The connection between European Union migration policy and Union citizenship policy is an under researched area.

It remains to be seen whether the divergence between the strengthening of internal mobility by the new Union citizenship directive, on the one hand, and the hesitant approach towards migration from third countries and these migrants' mobility rights within the Union, on the other hand, will be overcome in the near future. Although political documents suggest an approximation of legal statuses, the directives stop short of reaching this goal. This might also explain why the 2003 Communication suggests some moves with regard to naturalisation policies in order to overcome this stalemate. Analysing possible legal bases for Community action in this field and the position of Member States towards harmonisation of naturalisation policies will be the task of future research. The possibility to improve local political participation of immigrants under a Community legal framework also needs further analysis.

Text Box 6: Anne Walter, A right to family reunification

The recent harmonisation of rules on family reunification at the European level (Directive 2003/86/EC of 22 September 2003 on Family Reunification) reflects conflicts between, on the one hand, fundamental principles of protection for family life and, on the other hand, state interests to assert control over family reunification as a major component of the migration process. At present, national policies in the EU concerning families of third country nationals differ widely between human rights based and migration policy oriented approaches. This will not change after the implementation of the new harmonisation. A uniform right to a family unit throughout the EU seems to be rather a vision than reality. The directive only marginally harmonises the rules on family reunification and it allows for various concepts of family reunion.

Following the political recommendations of the Tampere European Council of October 1999, the initial draft of the family reunification directive for third country nationals proposed by the Commission was modelled on the basis of free-movement rules applicable to EU-citizens. Equal treatment of EU-citizens and nationals is the basic principle of integration in the EU. Consequently, the legal position of family members of EU-citizens (irrespective of their nationality) is also strongly derived from this principle of equal treatment. This will be reinforced with the implementation of the recent reform of the right to move freely within the EU for EU-citizens and families (Directive 2004/38/EC of 29 April 2004). However the ambitious goals of the Tampere programme clashed with the strong desire of certain Member States to control their gates of legal immigration. As a result, there are now two different EU-regimes for third country and EU-nationals. Contrary to the rules for EU-citizens those for third country nationals are non-binding and their flexibility is similar to an international agreement. Besides the lack of sufficient political consensus, the strong position of the Member States in the Council and the limited role of the European Parliament have hindered the development of common European family reunification standards. As a result, the standards contained in the directive are lower than those currently applied in many countries. The limited categories of persons covered, the minimum standards for entry and residence of family members and the numerous derogations may lead to a prolonged and sometimes permanent separation of families. These may well fall short of obligations all these states have subscribed to by signing the European Convention on Human Rights (ECHR) whose article 8 protects the right to private and family life. On the positive side, one must mention that standards are higher for refugees. There is, however, no reasonable justification why families of persons with subsidiary protection do not receive the same treatment as refugees. It is an open question whether the directive can fulfil its own objective to serve as an 'instrument of integration'. The notion of integration is mentioned several times in the directive, yet mostly in connection with restrictions and immigration criteria. In addition, Member States with a high level of protection can lower their standards, because the directive does not contain a general stand-still clause. For instance, the recent changes to the alien law in the Netherlands and France that have introduced restrictions on family reunification *in accordance with the directive* show that a future downgrading of national standards cannot be prevented.

Nevertheless, despite all criticism, it has to be recognised that family reunification found a general consensus and was regulated at the EU-level. Mechanisms of European legislation can now become a starting point for further evolution. The European Parliament's decision to challenge the Family Reunification Directive before the European Court of Justice for breach of human rights standards (its criticism of the Draft Directive were ignored during the legislation process) suggests that there is a good chance that the final outcome will be quite different from the original directive adopted by the Council. At the same time, it is also a powerful reminder of the Parliament's increasing role in shaping policies at EU level.

European citizenship and antidiscrimination

By introducing a new Article (Art. 13) into the TEC, the Treaty of Amsterdam for the first time empowered the European Union with competence in the field of fighting discrimination based on 'race' and ethnic origin (Bell 2002a,b, Geddes & Guiraudon 2002, Liegl, Perchinig & Weyss 2004: 13-17). This change was achieved after NGOs working in the field of migrants' rights (Chopin & Niessen 2001) and the European Parliament had exerted pressure. Despite previous deferments by some Member States, in 2002 the Council agreed upon two directives implementing measures against discrimination based on ethnic origin – the Racial Equality Directive[15] and the Employment Equality Directive[16]. The rather quick adoption of these directives was ironically accelerated by the inclusion of the extreme right-wing Freedom Party into government in Austria and the subsequent diplomatic ostracism against Austria (Tyson 2001).

> The question whether and how public discourse on antidiscrimination influences the understanding of European integration deserves further attention. In particular, it will be interesting to see whether the concept will become a relevant tool in the fight against discrimination based on nationality.

Although they differ in scope – discrimination outside working life is only prohibited with regard to 'race' and ethnic origin –, both directives provide protection against four different forms of discrimination: direct and indirect discrimination, discriminatory harassment, and instruction to discriminate. The wording of the directive – 'on grounds of' – indicates that the prohibition of discrimination also applies to so-called perceived characteristics, which gives the directive a wide material scope. Indirect discrimination is defined as a situation where an apparently neutral provision, criterion or practice puts persons with a certain racial or ethnic origin or religion or belief at a disparate/disproportionate disadvantage compared with other persons. The protection against discrimination conferred by the directives applies to all persons who are on the territory of one of the EU Member States, irrespective of their nationality (Liegl et al. 2004: 9). These provisions might open the door for an eventual inclusion of discrimination based on nationality in the interpretation of 'indirect discrimination'. Despite the reluctance of the Member States to implement the directives, it is likely that subsequent decisions of the ECJ will harmonise the protection against racial discrimination and discrimination based on ethnic origin in the coming years.

Apart from its legal aspects, the discourse on antidiscrimination has massively influenced European Union policy making in the field of employment policies. In 2003, measures against discrimination of third country nationals have been defined as a target of the Employment Guidelines and the Lisbon Strategy and more than half of the projects within the ESF-funded programme 'EQUAL' dealt with issues of staff diversity, including antidiscrimination and integration of immigrants. The implementation of antidiscrimination measures also is a major point in the ongoing debate on European Corporate Responsibility Standards (cf. Liegl et al. 2004: 50ff.).

The exclusion of discrimination based on nationality and the different scopes of protection in the directives remain the main weaknesses of EU-antidiscrimination regulations. Future research will have to examine the usage of the concept of indirect discrimination at European and Member State levels and its potential to prevent discrimination based on nationality. Furthermore, thorough studies on the adequacy and efficiency of the implementation system will be necessary to develop clear criteria for evaluating the quality of antidiscrimination systems (Perchinig 2003).

The concept of civic citizenship

The concept of civic citizenship[17] was first introduced in 2000 in a Communication of the Commission: 'The legal status granted to third country nationals would be based on the principle of providing sets of rights and responsibilities on a basis of equality with those of nationals but differentiated according to the length of stay while providing for progression to permanent status. In the longer term this could extend to offering a form of civic citizenship, based on the EC Treaty and inspired by the Charter of Fundamental Rights, consisting of a set of rights and duties offered to third country nationals' (COM (2000) 757 final: 21).

This idea was re-emphasised in several consecutive documents, particularly in the 2003 Communication on Immigration, Integration and Employment (COM (2003) 336 final), which demanded a holistic integration strategy fusing the European Employment Strategy, civic citizenship and nationality, and the fight against discrimination into an integrated concept aimed at managing, not preventing, migration. The Commission also linked the idea of civic citizenship to a suggested improvement of political participation at the local level for third country nationals, thus bringing the neglected issue of local voting rights for

> The suggested introduction of a 'European status' for third country nationals via the concept of civic citizenship deserves attention. The concept, which stresses the prohibition of discrimination based on nationality and the right to vote at local level, might be the missing link between Union citizenship, antidiscrimination policy and EU migration policies.

third country nationals back into integration policies. Furthermore, it commented for the first time on naturalisation policies, suggesting automatic or semi-automatic access to nationality for the second and third generation of immigrant descent. For the rights to be included in civic citizenship, the Commission pointed to the Charter of Fundamental Rights as a reference text (COM (2003) 336 final: 23). It might therefore be interesting to examine these rights conferred to Union citizens by the Charter.

Basically, they include the right to seek employment and to residence (Art. 15.2 and Art. 45), which has been reinforced by the recent directive consolidating Union citizenship, the prohibition of discrimination based on nationality (Art. 21.2), diplomatic and consular protection (Art. 46), and voting rights at municipal level and for the EP (Art. 39 and 40). The rights of access to documents and to petition the European Parliament and the European Ombudsman (Art. 42, 43 and 44) are not limited to Union Citizens but apply to any natural or legal person residing or having his or her registered office in a Member State.

Notwithstanding the antidiscrimination directives and the directive on the status of long-term residents, third country nationals do not enjoy the same level of residence rights as Union citizens. They are not protected against discrimination based on nationality and do not have voting rights at the local level and to the European Parliament. An extension of these rights to third country nationals as envisaged in the Communication could close the gaps in the antidiscrimination directives and the directive on long-term residents. An equalisation of residence rights would automatically also include harmonisation with regard to the right to family reunification. Thus the concept of 'civic citizenship' could become a tool for gradually harmonising the status of third country nationals with Union citizens and guaranteeing a common legal status for immigrants in all Member States. It could finally question the still existing nexus between Member State nationality and European citizenship. Nevertheless, major political rights – the right to vote at national level – and access to all public offices would still be withheld, so the core of this nexus would stay untouched. Despite this caveat, the introduction of a specific 'European' status for third country nationals could in future open a new dynamic towards eventually extending political rights for Union and civic citizens to the provincial or even national level.

'One cannot, conceptually and psychologically (let alone legally) be a European citizen without being a Member State national', J. H. H. Weiler stated in his famous 1997 Jean Monnet Lecture at the London School of Economics (Weiler 1997: 510). Weiler interprets European citizenship as bridging the national and supranational, 'eros and civilisation', in a way that allows 'nationality and statism to thrive, their demonic aspects under civilizatory constraints' (Weiler 1997: 511). Whereas Habermas' concept of constitutional patriotism stays bound to the nation state, seeking to tame nationality by constitutional reason, Weiler transfers this task to Union citizenship. The concept of civic citizenship even goes a step further and uncouples Union citizenship from Member State nationality. This might be an indication that in future civilisation could prevail, confining Eros to its ancestral realm: the private sphere. Suggesting an extension of the legal status of third country nationals to those of Union citizens without requiring that they belong to a Member State, the concept might also question the still existing link between nationality and Union citizenship and thus become a tool for the development of a true Union citizenship deserving of its name. This enlightened approach to Europe, in which rights would be based on residency, not nationality, might well have the potential to overcome the state-boundedness of naturalisation (Kostakopoulou 2003). European citizens would then no longer have to carry the burden of a Member State nationality. Thus civic citizenship might have the potential of reaching beyond nationality-based measures of political integration, such as the toleration of dual nationality. Nevertheless, the concept currently still is as vague as the first concepts of European citizenship have been, and it is not at all clear whether civic citizenship is regarded as an interim status before naturalisation or as a permanent legal status conferred and withdrawn directly by European Union institutions.

The idea therefore opens new perspectives for research, ranging from the historical analysis of the concept of citizenship of residence (ius domicili), the linkage with developments in the field of Member State nationality policies or in the field of human rights to questions regarding the future institutional design of the European Union polity.

4 Political participation, mobilisation and representation of immigrants and their offspring in Europe

Marco Martiniello

Introduction

In many EU countries, political mobilisation, participation and representation of immigrants and their offspring were for a long time not considered to be important issues both in academia and in politics. Immigrant workers were not regarded as potential citizens. They were not supposed and expected to be politically active. As guests, they were even asked to observe a kind of 'devoir de réserve'. In other words, they were invited not to interfere with their hosts' political and collective affairs. Migrants had only an economic role in the host society: to work and to produce.

This has changed, at least in those European countries that have already faced several waves of immigration in the past five decades. Here, political mobilisation, participation and representation of ethnic immigrant minorities have become topical issues especially at the local and city levels. The sensitive debates about the integration of immigrants cannot exclude this political dimension.

> We now have a reasonably good knowledge of immigrants' political activities but some gaps remain to be filled.

This chapter is not a bibliographical review of the European literature on political participation, mobilisation and representation of immigrants. Its aim is rather to provide a qualitative overview of the state of the art on these issues and also to present some research perspectives to be explored in the future. As a matter of fact, we now have a reasonably good knowledge of immigrants' political activities but some gaps remain to be filled. The chapter is divided into six parts. The first part addresses very briefly conceptual and definition issues. The second part presents and discusses the earliest major hypothesis to be historically found in the literature, namely, the thesis of political quiescence of immigrants. The third part focuses on the explanations of the various forms of immigrant political participation. The fourth part presents a typology of immigrant political participation in the country of settlement. This typology serves to map areas for further research. The fifth part discusses specifically the issue of transnational political participation. The sixth part identifies a few gaps in the literature to which new research perspectives could correspond. Finally, the concluding policy-oriented part will address the issue of how to evaluate and assess political participation of immigrants and their offspring in the country of residence.

Definitions and concepts

As is often the case in social sciences, discussions about concepts and definitions can be endless. The aim here is not to solve the academic disputes but simply to clarify how we will use specific expressions in this report.

Immigrants' political integration involves political participation, mobilisation and representation.

In a broad sense, political integration contains four dimensions. The first dimension refers to the rights granted to immigrants by the host society. One could say that the more political rights they get the better they are integrated. The second dimension is their identification with the host society. The more immigrants identify with the host society the better their political integration. The third dimension refers to the adoption of democratic norms and values by the immigrants, which is often presented as a necessary condition for political integration. Finally, immigrants' political integration involves political participation, mobilisation and representation, which are the core issues discussed in this chapter.

Political participation is understood as the active dimension of citizenship. It refers to the various ways in which individuals take part in the management of collective affairs of a given political community. Political participation cannot be restricted, as much political science research is, to conventional forms such as voting or running for election. It also covers other and less conventional types of political activities such as protests, demonstrations, sit-ins, hunger strikes, boycotts, etc.

Even though the distinction between conventional and less conventional forms of political participation is a matter of discussion among political scientists, we claim that it is useful since the two categories involve different patterns of activities.

Apart from the level of 'conventionality', i.e. the degree to which a form of political participation is conventional, there is another important distinction. Less conventional and extra-parliamentary forms of political participation are most often relevant when they are collective. They presuppose in most cases the constitution of a collective actor characterised by a collective identity and some degree of organisation through a *mobilisation* process. In a narrow sense, *political mobilisation* refers precisely to the process of building collective actors and collective identity. By contrast, conventional forms of political participation, while not excluding comparable patterns of mobilisation, take place within a previously structured set of political institutions. This allows for individual political participation. Making a demonstration on your own does not generally make much political sense while voting can be interpreted as a very personal contribution to the functioning of a political community. (Every single vote counts!) Voting can, however, also be seen as a collective action when groups of voters organise a bloc voting initiative that needs mobilisation. Conversely, some unconventional forms of political participation, such as hunger strikes, may occasionally also be articulated as individual protest.

In other words, the distinction between conventional and less conventional forms of political participation and the distinction between individual and collective political participation are neither totally sharp nor do they overlap perfectly. Conventional political participation can be both personal and collective while less conventional forms of political participation are in practice mostly collective and therefore the result of a process of mobilisation.

Political representation can be understood in two ways. Firstly, in modern democracies, power is usually exercised by a group of persons whose legitimacy to govern has its source in free elections. Through the vote, the citizens mandate those persons to govern on their behalf. This process of legitimisation of government action is called political representation. But secondly, political representation also refers to the result of the legitimisation process, namely the group of people mandated to govern on behalf of the citizens.

The thesis of political quiescence of immigrants

In European literature on immigration, the thesis of the political quiescence or passivity of immigrants was the first to emerge and it was for a long time dominant. Migrant workers were considered to be apolitical and characterised by political apathy (Martiniello 1997).

This thesis was shared both by Marxist and non-Marxist scholars. The point of departure was correct. In many countries, migrant workers had virtually no political rights. They could neither vote nor be elected. They did not enjoy any form of direct political representation within political institutions.

> For a long time, migrant workers were considered to be apolitical and characterised by political apathy.

According to some scholars, this exclusion from the electoral process prevented migrants from playing any relevant political role in the country of residence and explained their political apathy. Apart from being formally disenfranchised, migrants were also seen to be so strongly oriented towards achieving short-term economic goals that they would not be interested in political participation.

Other scholars saw the political passivity of migrants as the result of their lack of political and democratic culture due to the political history of their countries of origin, which were either under an authoritarian regime or had only recently democratised.

The first explanation, which was mainly put forward by Marxists, was partially correct but it was flawed in two ways. First, as mentioned above, relevant political participation cannot be reduced to electoral participation. Other important forms such as trade union politics, associations and community organisation have to be taken into account as well. Many studies show that immigrants have always been active in those less conventional types of participation. Second, the explanation tends to consider the migrant only as a worker, as a factor of production whose life is totally determined by macro-economic and macro-social structures. It therefore leaves no place for agency or autonomy and dehumanises migrant workers in this respect. This is a reason why many Marxist scholars were more interested in emphasising how migrants were used to divide and demobilise the working class struggles than in studying immigrants' political activities.

The second explanation mainly put forward by non-Marxist scholars reflected a culturalist and paternalistic approach. The view was that migrants were less culturally developed than local workers and therefore also less politically active. This interpretation was clearly problematic and refuted by facts. In many cases, migrant workers were actually politicised in their country of origin before their departure and migration was a way to escape dictatorship. Immigrants from Italy during fascism, from Spain during francism and from Greece during the colonels' regime are good illustrations of immigrants arriving with a strong political culture and democratic aspirations.

Furthermore, both explanations seem to confuse quiescence or passivity and apolitical attitudes. Being politically passive is not always an indicator of general disinterest in politics. Passivity can sometimes be a form of resistance and defence. When political opportunities are very limited and avenues of political participation strictly restricted and controlled, passivity can be a transitional waiting position for better days, for more open opportunities for participation.

> Migrants are not more passive than other citizens but their involvement should also not be exaggerated by regarding them as the vanguard of the new global proletariat.

In any case, the two variants of the migrant quiescence thesis have been strongly challenged by facts. Migrants have always been involved in politics either outside or at the margins of the political system of both their country of origin and their country of residence. More recently, migrants and their offspring have become more strongly involved in the mainstream political institutions. This process has been facilitated by an extension of the voting rights to foreigners in several countries and by a liberalisation of nationality laws in others. Migrants are not more passive than other citizens but their involvement should also not be exaggerated by regarding them as 'an emerging political force' (Miller 1981) or as the vanguard of the new global proletariat.

Explaining the various forms of immigrant political participation

Political science and political sociology have tried to explain political participation in many different ways. Theories of political participation abound and each gives its own answer to the question: why do people participate in politics? Traditionally, there was a dispute between rational choice and identity approaches to political participation. More recently, scholars have also tried to explain the decline of political participation and the retreat of many citizens toward their private space in many democracies. These general issues are obviously very complex.

They are just as complex when applied specifically to migrant and migrant origin populations. However if we accept the idea that there is always some degree of political participation amongst immigrant populations, we can concentrate on explaining the various forms this participation takes. This will focus attention on questions such as the following: How to explain political mobilisation of immigrants outside the mainstream political institutions? How to explain the variable intensity of immigrants' political participation? How to explain the direction of political participation towards the host society or towards the country of origin or towards a global political space? How to explain strategies of individual migrants who engage in a personal political career in formal political institutions? How to explain the salience or weakness of union politics for migrants? How to explain the success or failure of consultative politics?

> The forms of immigrants' political participation largely and firstly depend on the structure of political opportunities present at a given time and in a given society.

In order to answer that type of questions, it is suggested that the forms of immigrants' political participation largely and firstly depend on the structure of political opportunities present at a given time and in a given society, which is the result of inclusion-exclusion mechanisms developed by the states (of residence and of origin) and their political systems (Martiniello 1998).

By granting or denying voting rights to foreigners, by facilitating or impeding access to citizenship and nationality, by granting or constraining freedom of association, by ensuring or blocking the representation of migrants' interests, by establishing or not establishing arenas and institutions for consultative politics, states open or close avenues of political participation for migrants and provide them with more or less opportunities to participate in the management of collective affairs.

Whether immigrants and their offspring will seize these opportunities in this changing institutionally defined framework will depend on several variables such as: their political ideas and values, their previous involvement in politics (including experiences in the country of origin), the degree of 'institutional completeness' of the immigrant ethnic community, the vision they have of their presence in the country of residence as permanent or temporary, their feeling of belonging to the host and/or their society of origin, their knowledge of the political system and institutions, the social capital and density of immigrant associational networks[1], plus all the usual determinants of political behaviour such as level of education, linguistic skills, socio-economic status, gender, age or generational cohort. Migrants can also mobilise to try and open up new avenues of political participation. We then will have to consider how the various theories on collective action apply to their mobilisation.

Recently, academic interest in political participation of migrants has been connected to a renewed interest in citizenship, though the latter is clearly not the same in all EU Member States and in the US.

In France, a lot of work has been done on second-generation immigrants' extra-parliamentary mobilisation in the 1980s. Some studies have been made on the importance of ethnicity in the political system.

Let us mention the work by Sylvie Strudel on Jews in French political life in which she deals with the hypothesis of the existence of a Jewish vote (Strudel 1996). The work of Vincent Geisser (1997) needs also to be mentioned. He is the author of one of the first studies on immigrant local councillors in France. One of the most prolific authors on immigrants and politics in France is Catherine Withol de Wenden (1988). In the 1990s the *sans-papiers* movement was extensively studied (Simeant 1997) and very recently the religious-political mobilisation around the issues of the headscarf, and more generally the evolution of secularism (laïcité), has drawn much attention.

In the UK, the issue of electoral power of ethnic minorities as well as the political colour of each ethnic minority is discussed in all elections. Historically, West Indians and Asians were largely pro-Labour but recently their votes have become a little more evenly distributed across parties. The issue of the representation of minorities in elected assemblies has also been studied by scholars such as Geddes (1998) and Saggar (1998).

In the Netherlands and in Scandinavia there have been precise studies on the electoral behavior of immigrants led by Tillie (1998) and Fennema in the Netherlands (also see text box 7 below) and Soininen (1999) in Sweden. In the latter country, studies also tried to explain the decline of immigrant voter turnout in local elections over the past decade. There is very little comparable research of this kind in other EU Member States.

Text Box 7: Anja Van Heelsum, Research on voting behaviour of ethnic groups in the Netherlands

Ethnic minority groups tend to have a lower turnout rate in elections than the Dutch. Tillie (in 1994), Van Heelsum & Tillie (in 1998) and Michon & Tillie (in 2002) held exit polls during the municipal elections. The following table shows the turnout rates:

Turn out rates of five ethnic groups at the local elections of 1994, 1998 and 2002 in per cent of the respective ethnic local population

Background	Amsterdam			Rotterdam		The Hague		Utrecht		Arnhem	
	1994	1998	2002	1994	1998	1994	1998	1994	1998	1994	1998
Turks	67	39	30	28	42	-*	36	55	39	56	50
Moroccans	49	23	22	23	33	-	23	44	26	51	18
Surinamese/ Antilleans	30	21	26	24	25	-	27	-	22	-	20
Cape Verdians	-	-	-	34	33	-	-	-	-	-	-
City turnout	56,8	45,7	47,8	56,9	48,4	57,6	57,6	59,8	56,5	57,2	52,0

* The Hague 1994: no data

> Turks show higher turnout than Surinamese and Moroccans, but throughout the years there is a dramatic decline in the number of people from ethnic minority groups. Most of the ethnic minority voting is on the left of the political spectrum. About 50 per cent of the ethnic minorities vote on the socialist party and about 20 per cent vote on the Green Left. This is probably due to a more immigrant friendly attitude of these parties.

A typology of the various forms of immigrant political participation in the country of settlement

This section of the chapter suggests a typology that is limited to all means of legal political participation, excluding the various forms of terrorism and political violence and corruption. However, examples of terrorist actions and political violence are to be found in the history of immigration in Europe. In the Netherlands, in the 1970s a group of Molluccans 'rail-jacked' a train and took the passengers as hostages. In Belgium, the UK and France, riots and urban violence in which migrants or subsequent generations were involved can certainly also be analysed in political terms (e.g. the Brussels riots in 1991, the 2001 riots in Bradford, Oldham and Burnley or the urban unrest in various French banlieues in the 1980s and 1990s). Although the actors on the street in these events may not have been consciously politically motivated, their actions certainly had a strong political impact.

> Different types of ethnic politics or immigrant political participation can be distinguished according to the geographic-political level of action and the level of conventionality.

Different types of ethnic politics or immigrant political participation can be distinguished according to the geographic-political level of action and the level of conventionality, i.e. the contrast between state and non-state politics.

The geographic-political level of action

The nation state is certainly an imperfect and vulnerable form of political organisation. It currently faces both internal and external problems. On the one hand, internal regionalisms and sub-nationalisms seem to be rising in several European nation states questioning seriously the sovereignty of the 'centre'. Italy, the United Kingdom, Spain, Belgium, among others, are concerned with this type of difficulties. On the other hand, new supranational forces represent without any doubt a challenge to the nation state in its present form. The emergence of supranational power blocs like the European Union, the rise of transnational corporations, but also of mass telecommunication systems and other new technologies stimulate a debate about the possible demise of the nation state. Still, despite all these problems, the nation state remains a crucial setting and framework for political action. In this respect, immigrant political participation can theoretically be envisaged both in the country of residence and in the country of origin of the migrants.

Apart from at the central level in each European nation state, political action can also take place at different infra-nation state levels, going from the neighbourhood to the region. In this respect each political system has its own specific organisation. Consequently, the expression 'local politics' does not have the same meaning in every country. Still, opportunities of participation and mobilisation exist at all local and regional levels (district, town, municipality, county, land, region, province, canton, department, etc.).

If we turn to the supra-national level, the 1992 Maastricht Treaty has provided a new impetus for the construction of a European Political Union. The problems to be solved are still numerous as shown by the current debate about the EU Constitutional Treaty, and the final geographic shape of this regional power bloc has not yet been fully specified. However migrant political action certainly occurs at the European Union level, too. Furthermore, there is no reason why the EU should constitute the geographic-political limit for such action. It can eventually extend to the world level, as for example in the anti-globalisation movement.

State politics and non-state politics

The distinction between state and non-state politics covers approximately the distinction between conventional and non-conventional politics presented above. The concept of state is used here in a narrow sense to refer to the set of formal political institutions that form the core of executive, legislative and judiciary powers. Beyond the state, the polity is also made up of other political institutions and actors who, at least in a democracy, take part in one way or another in the definition and the management of society's collective affairs.

As far as *state politics* is concerned, three main forms of ethnic participation and mobilisation can be considered, namely electoral politics, parliamentary politics and consultative politics.

Electoral politics
The issue of a black and ethnic vote has been discussed for a long time in the United States. In Europe, one of the first studies on the importance of the 'black vote' was carried out by the Community Relations Commission during the British general elections of 1974 (Solomos & Back 1991). Since then, there has been a growing interest among political parties in gathering support from ethnic and black communities.

It is important to underline that in nearly all European states but also in non-European democracies full electoral rights are reserved for the countries' nationals[2] even though some of them have enfranchised aliens at the local level (see table 2 in the annex). Therefore, legal obstacles to ethnic electoral participation are essentially determined by rules for access to citizenship through ius soli or naturalisation.

> There is no convincing general theory that would explain a link between ethnic and racial belonging and political behaviour in general or electoral behaviour in particular.

Recently, the issue of an ethnic vote in different EU countries and in the US has attracted a lot of attention and provoked some sort of panic. The question has been extensively studied by American political scientists since the Voting Rights Act of 1965, which created a new electorate by removing discriminatory laws intended to prevent Black Americans from voting, even though their formal right to vote existed long before that date. However, up to now, there is no convincing general theory that would explain a link between ethnic and racial belonging and political behaviour in general or electoral behaviour in particular. The existence of an ethnically or racially motivated vote remains dubious. Nevertheless, with each election, common sense requires the need for each candidate who enters the race to win the votes of Jews, Blacks, Hispanics and more and more frequently also of sexual minorities.

Consequently, the ethnic vote should always be treated as a contingent phenomenon in need of explanation rather than as a presupposition that relies on the dubious assumption that ethnic groups tend to cast block votes. The research task consists in studying the factors and the circumstances likely to promote and explain the development of an electoral behaviour that is specific to an electorate that supposedly belongs to an ethnic category, in this case the electorate of immigrant origin. There are basically two sets of factors whose interplay will determine the emergence of an ethnic vote: first, residential concentration, density of social networks, shared experiences of discrimination, and the formation of political elites within an immigrant population; and, second, features of the electoral system such as voter registration rules, majoritarian or proportional representation voting systems, rules for determining electoral districts ('gerrymandering' or affirmative representation of minorities), etc.

Moreover, the ethnic or immigrant vote should be clearly defined. In a first sense, it refers to the individual vote cast by a voter who belongs to an ethnic category for one or several candidates of the same ethnic group, or for a party which regroups candidates of this same group. These candidates or parties are considered by the voter as her automatic representatives because of their shared ethnic belonging. The latter is sufficient to account for the expressed vote whatever the political programme proposed. In a second and broader sense, we can also talk of an ethnic vote when a substantial majority of voters of a same ethnic category support a specific candidate or party and their policy whatever the ethnic origin of the candidate or composition of the party.[3] Such collective or block voting may be subjected to some bargaining between the electors and the candidates, the latter promising to give a particular advantage to the group in exchange for their votes. This vote can also result from the subjective awareness of the group that this candidate or this party better understands the concerns of the ethnic category and is likely to defend their interests. This distinction is clearly theoretical. Indeed, it is easy to imagine cases where the vote could simultaneously become ethnic in both meanings described above. It should nevertheless be stressed that a voter with an ethnic background does not necessarily – by nature so to say – cast an 'ethnic vote' in either of the two meanings considered above.

> We do not know precisely how immigrant citizens of Muslim origin vote in all the Member States of the EU.

In Europe the issue that has recently been prominent on the political agenda is the potential emergence of an Islamic vote amongst immigrant populations, but we do not know precisely how immigrant citizens of Muslim origin vote in all the Member States of the EU. There are studies on the electoral behaviour of Muslim citizens in some countries, but researchers in others with a strong presence of Muslim migrants have not yet addressed this question or lack an adequate data base for doing so. Furthermore, although there are many Islamic associations, the Islamic parties created in different EU countries have so far not been able to gain seats in parliamentary and local elections with probably a few local exceptions. This tends to show that thus far Muslim citizens have generally voted for traditional mainstream parties.

Parliamentary politics

The representation of ethnic minorities in the central government, parliament and local government is also an increasingly important issue, especially in those countries that have long-established immigrant populations, such as the United Kingdom, Belgium, France, and the Netherlands.

> The representation of ethnic minorities in the central government, parliament and local government is an increasingly important issue.

There are different levels and questions of research in this area. Political philosophers and normative theorists consider whether ethnic minorities have claims to special representation in order to offset disadvantages they face as discriminated groups in society or as 'permanent minorities' whose concerns risk being consistently overruled in majoritarian decisions. This type of argument must, however, overcome a well-established critique of 'descriptive representation' models according to which representative assemblies should mirror the composition of the wider society (see, for example, Pitkin (1967) and Phillips (1995)). Political scientists study how ethnic diversity affects the internal working of parliamentary assemblies and parties, e.g. the emergence of ethnic caucuses or cross-party voting on ethnic issues. Sociologists examine the role of immigrant and ethnic minority politicians: to what extent do they differ from mainstream politicians in terms of their agenda and their mode of functioning?.

Consultative politics

Electoral politics and parliamentary assemblies are not the only arenas for ethnic political participation. Some states have created consultative institutions at the periphery of the state to deal with ethnic categories and immigration problems. Usually, these bodies have only little power, for example as advisory boards. Among the earliest examples of this were the Belgian 'Conseils Consultatifs Communaux pour les immigrés' that were established in the late sixties in several cities (Martiniello 1992).

Text Box 8: Davide Però, The 'comedy' of participation: immigrant consultation in southern European cities

Can consultation mechanisms substitute for a lack of direct representation of immigrants at the local level? Local voting rights for third country nationals are more common in Western and Northern Europe than in the comparatively new immigration states of the

Mediterranean. Ethnographic research in the cities of Barcelona and Bologna has examined how local officials, NGOs and immigrants perceive opportunities for immigrant political participation and representation.

Some local officials consider 'integration' possible without voting rights, and some even regard such rights as dangerous because they see immigrants as lacking the necessary pre-requisites to be allowed full participation in the democratic process. As one representative from the Catalan nationalist Government put it 'they cannot really understand the history of oppression of the Catalan people', or, as one Left Democrat militant in Bologna said, 'they are not accustomed to democracy'.

In this context, participation in governance for immigrants takes two forms. The first is participation in policy implementation by proxy. In this way, immigrants are represented through the autochthonous 'pro-immigrant' NGOs that the local authorities hire to deliver services to immigrants. The second form is participation in token consultative institutions like the Consell of Barcelona or the Forum of Bologna. These bodies rarely meet their immigrant participants' needs. On their effectiveness there is a striking similarity between the immigrants' views in the two cities. One participant in the Barcelona Consell asked: 'If decisions and interventions are made unilaterally by the City Council that decides what to do all by itself, then what do we have a Consell for? ...If the Consell does not meet when concrete events are occurring then what's the point of having such Consell? ...Then its meetings are a pure comedy, a pure and dramatic comedy'. In Bologna: 'The Council and its officials need interlocutors and legitimisation. They do not really think that the associations [of the Forum] are representative, but these are those who have agreed to play a role in the comedy'.

What all this suggests is that participation and empowerment deriving from these consultative bodies are greater for local governments and the autochthonous NGOs than they are for immigrants. The first gain legitimisation and a politically correct image, the second are being contracted for the delivery of public services, while the third are often politically neutralised and excluded.

Political scientists have generally criticised the idea of special consultative bodies for immigrants for marginalising immigrants further while giving them the illusion of direct political participation However, recently, a new initiative from the Council of Europe put the issue on the table again (Gsir & Martiniello 2004). There are hundreds of consultative bodies across Europe. The idea of the Council of Europe is to develop a manual of common principles and guidelines in the area of consultation that could be used by the cities interested in creating some form of consultative body for immigrants.

As far as *non-state politics* is concerned, four main avenues of ethnic and immigrant political participation and mobilisation can be singled out: involvement in political parties, in union politics, in other pressure groups, and the direct mobilisation of ethnic communities.

Involvement in political parties

In democratic states, political parties are located at the intersection between civil society and state institutions. Their role is to translate societal interests and ideologies into legislative inputs and to train and select the personnel for political offices. Party politics is therefore an element of conventional politics. However, democratic parties are also voluntary associations rather than state institutions that exercise legitimate political authority. Moreover, not all political parties are represented in legislative assemblies. Some stay at the margin of the political system where they often campaign for more radical political change.

In Europe, the issue of ethnic involvement in political parties emerged first in Britain with the debate about the Black section in the Labour Party in the 1980s. On the continent, the development of the association France Plus gave another dimension to the problem, which could be very sensitive in the future in other countries as well. Its strategy was to encourage immigrants to join all democratic parties and to negotiate their electoral support on the basis of the advantages promised by each of the parties.

Union politics

The presence of immigrants in unions is an older and better known phenomenon. One could say that union politics is the cradle of immigrants' political participation. However, it is important to remark that the various European and American unions responded in different ways to the ethnic issue. Some organised specific institutions for 'migrant workers' within the union while others refused to do so in the name of the unity of the working class. Anyway, the decline of unions all over Europe is a crucial dimension to take into account when studying ethnic participation and mobilisation.

Union politics is the cradle of immigrants' political participation.

Other pressure groups

Immigrants can also get involved, as the other citizens, in all kinds of pressure groups and movements defending a great variety of interests. Let's mention here the *sans-papiers* movements across the US and Europe in which several unconventional types of action are used, such as hunger strikes or occupation of churches. Immigrants, as any other citizens, can also be involved in environmentalist movements, in animal rights groups or similar initiatives.

Ethnic community mobilisation

In order to promote and defend political interests and to exert some pressure on the political system, immigrant groups can organise as collective actors along ethnic, racial or religious lines. In recent years, the mobilisation of Muslim immigrants around religious concerns has received wide attention even though it is only one amongst many other forms of ethnic political mobilisation.

Combining the three geographic-political levels of action and different avenues of participation and mobilisation in conventional and non-conventional politics generates 21 potential arenas for political action. Obviously, not each of these can or should be studied separately. The goal of this typology is rather to indicate the scope and variety of immigrant participation within destination countries.

Text Box 9: Anja Van Heelsum, Research on civic participation in the Netherlands

Associations of immigrants can play an important role in integration processes. Van Heelsum (2004a, b) and Penninx and Van Heelsum (2004) investigated the number of associations and their functioning within minority communities and in relation to the political opportunity structure. A major reason why community organisations are established is to reach a political, religious, social, sports or any kind of common goal. An association is itself a network of people that can spread information. Immigrant associations also easily become part of a larger network, for instance with the city authorities and welfare institutions. Isolated individuals are reached and activated to join in gatherings and to voice their demands. The Dutch opportunity structure favours religious organisation, as a result of the pillarised structure that already existed. This is why Islamic and Hindu schools and broadcasting organisations have been established. Within the Turkish, Moroccan, Surinamese and African communities religious associations outnumber other types of associations. Within the Somali and Moluccan community developmental aid is the most common type. About one third of these associations are financially or otherwise supported by authorities. The organisational density varies among the different minority communities as the following table shows.

Population, number of associations and organisational density per ethnic group, ordered by organisational density

ethnic group	population in the Netherlands *	number of associations	organisational density (= associations/ inhabitants x 1000)
Afghans	34.000	34	1,0
Vietnamese	17.000	28	1,7
Iraqi	42.000	18	
Iranian	28.000	31	
Kurds	?	98	2,1
Tamils (Sri Lanka)	7.000	17	2,4
Moroccans	295.000	720	2,4
Surinamese	321.000	881	2,7
Turks	341.000	1125	3,3
Bosnians	11.000	44	4,0
Congolese (DR Congo, former Zaire)	7.000	35	5,0
Somalis	28.000	161	5,8
Chinese	39.000	244	6,3
Ethiopians		34	
Eritreans	10.000	42	7,6
Moluccans	40.000	399	9,9

* On 1 January 2003 (CBS 2003: 116) or Van den Tillaart, Olde Monnikhof, van den Berg & Warmerdam (2000: 28).

Transnational political participation

Globalisation, cosmopolitanism, post-nationalism and transnationalism have become key words in social sciences in general and in migration, ethnic and citizenship studies in particular, since the early 1990s. As far as transnationalism is concerned, research projects and programmes like the Transnational Communities Programme at Oxford have developed. Numerous conferences have been organised. New journals, such as Global Networks, have been launched. Many scholars have undoubtedly been attracted by the transnationalism discourse but many others have also been very critical about what they see as just another fashion in social sciences.

The concept of 'immigrant transnationalism' was introduced in the literature by a group of female anthropologists in 1992. When Nina

Glick Schiller, Linda Basch and Cristina Blanc-Szanton published their book *Towards a Transnational Perspective on Migration*, they opened the way for the development of new discussions and debates in ethnic and migration studies on transnationalism.

Since then, the number of understandings, concepts and definitions of transnationalism has exploded to the extent that it is not easy to know exactly what scholars talk about when they write about transnationalism.

It has often been argued that globalisation has implied, or indeed created, new patterns of migration (between but also within states) that differ fundamentally from traditional patterns of migrations such as 'guestworkers system' or chain migration. It is also often argued that these new patterns of migration lead to new mechanisms of transmigrant community building, to the emergence of new types of deterritorialised collective identities, to the growth of new forms of belonging that challenge the traditional nation-states belonging. These allegedly new developments are captured by the expressions transnational communities, post-national membership or new cosmopolitanism, to just mention a few.

In what is regarded as traditional migration processes, ethnic migrant communities were either trying to preserve their ethnic identity linked to the sending country or they were assimilating into the new society by abandoning their heritage and by adopting a new national identity. Alternatively, they could prepare their return to the country of origin or stay for good but still cling to a myth of return. All the traditional literature on migration is about these issues and processes. All in all, migrants were supposed to be given a choice between ethnic and national identities but at the end of the day, they were supposed to belong either to the country of origin or to the country of settlement. If they made the former choice, they were supposed to return. If they opted for the latter, they were supposed to change their political affiliation and eventually their citizenship.

In today's transmigrational processes things would be different. New communities of transmigrants in the global era would be closer to the ideal of world citizens. They would have become detached from ethnic and national bonds to embrace post-ethnic and post-national identities because of their transnational practices. They would have become transnational communities characterised by new forms of belonging and identities translating into transnational political practices. This view is not shared by all scholars using the concept of transnationalism but it is well represented in the literature.

Transnational activities and practices can be economic, political and socio-cultural. In the field of economics, transnational entrepreneurs mobilise their contacts across borders in search of goods and suppliers,

> Political transnational activities create links between countries of origin and destination and can be directed towards either of the two political systems.

of capital and markets. Economic transnationalism includes also remittances and investments made by migrants in the development of the country of origin. Transmigrants' economic activities can go in both directions between the country of origin and the country of residence. Socio-cultural transnational activities can be numerous and diverse. They include the election of expatriate beauty queens that compete in the home country contest, tours of folk music groups from the country of origin to perform for migrants in their country of residence, etc. Political transnational activities can take different forms, too. Transmigrants can mobilise in the country of residence to produce a political impact in the country of origin. Party leaders from the country of origin can travel to the countries of residence in order to gather electoral support in transmigrant communities. Sending countries can also try to intervene in the host countries by using immigrant communities as a resource to defend their interests.

At a higher level of abstraction, these transnational practices reveal a crucial change that has occurred with the globalisation of the economy, namely the passage for many people from a national to a transnational condition. Until not so long ago migrants were considered to be an anomaly in the nation-state framework. With the acceleration of globalisation, a new phenomenon has occurred, namely the creation of a transnational community linking immigrant groups in the advanced countries with their respective sending nations and hometowns. This defines the new transnational condition 'composed of a growing number of persons who live dual lives: speaking two languages, having homes in two countries, and making a living through continuous regular contacts across national borders' (Portes, Guarnizo & Landolt 1999).

> Immigrants' integration or incorporation in the host country and transnational practices can occur simultaneously.

The development of this new condition has been made possible by changes that have taken place within the broader phenomenon of globalisation: the revolution in technologies of communication, the reduction of the costs of travelling and the multiplication of means of travel.

The insights of the transnational approach or perspective are manifold. It acknowledges the fact that immigrants' integration or incorporation in the host country and transnational practices can occur simultaneoulsy. However more research is needed both at the theoretical and the empirical level, in particular to make sense of the impact of transnationalism on immigrants' political participation.

Research perspectives

> The gender dimension of immigrants' political participation has not sufficiently been explored.

There are several gaps in the literature on political participation of immigrants. Certainly progress in this area has been quite dramatic over the past decade but our knowledge remains fragmented and largely confined to specific national contexts. More specifically, the gender dimension of immigrants' political participation has not sufficiently been explored. Researchers should make an effort to integrate the theoretical framework and also to produce comparative data, quantitative as well as qualitative, both in the more traditional areas of research and in the newer ones.

> It would be interesting to design electoral surveys at the EU level to try to better understand how citizens with an immigrant or ethnic minority background vote.

Regarding the former, it would be interesting to design electoral surveys at the EU level to try to better understand how citizens with an immigrant or ethnic minority background vote. Their political attitudes also need to be better examined. A third direction would be to try to find out who votes for ethnic minority candidates in the various Member States of the EU. It would also be very stimulating to systematically analyse the gender dimension of immigrants' political participation by comparing the different immigrant groups in the same country but also by comparing different host societies. Finally, the possible link between access to nationality and political participation also calls for more studies.

Three main perspectives need to be developed:
a) The implications of transnational political participation of migrants and their offspring in Europe
   A theoretical as well as an empirical discussion on the links between transnational political participation of immigrants and citizenship,

both in the country of origin and of residence, is needed. What does it mean for an immigrant who has acquired the nationality of the country of residence to participate politically in the country of origin? How does this affect the common understanding of nationality in the wider society? Can one be an active citizen in more than one polity? What is the impact of such double participation on identity and belonging? The questions have to a certain extent already been raised and researched in some countries for specific groups of immigrants but a lot still needs to be done.

b) The links between religion and political participation in post-migration situations

In several EU Member States, new Islamic parties have recently appeared. In many cases they are formed by citizens of immigrant origin or by local converts. In most instances, these parties have not so far gained a dramatic electoral success. Nevertheless, in the present context they reveal new developments concerning the links between religion and politics for immigrants and their offspring.

c) The rise of virtual ethnic and immigrant political communities

Internet opens up new channels of political mobilisation across state boundaries. The new electronic media may be a potent resource for immigrants engaged in transnational political activities across different destination countries or between sending and receiving states. We still don't know very precisely how immigrants use the internet for political purposes. Attention has so far focused on global terrorism, while non-violent ways of using the internet have been neglected.

How to evaluate political participation of immigrants and their offspring in the country of residence?

The task of constructing indicators of political participation of immigrants and their offspring that would allow for comparison, ranking and benchmarking across the EU faces several difficulties. The first difficulty refers to the variety of citizenship (nationality) laws and policies in the Member States of the EU discussed in chapter 2 of this report (see table 1 in the annex). Rules of access and loss of citizenship impact directly on opportunities to participate in formal political life and determine which institutions are open to immigrants and their offspring. When access to citizenship is easy, immigrants are not excluded from the right to take part in formal political life although many may still choose not to naturalise and will then remain excluded from rights of vote and eligibility. The more difficult and restricted access to citizenship is, the more immigrants are confined to non-conventional forms of political participation. Apart from rules of admission to citizenship, there is a similar variety with regard to political rights and opportunities for participation for non-citizen residents. As mentioned above, several EU Member States grant local voting rights to all foreigners while others limit them to EU citizens (see table 2 in the annex). These different legal frameworks make it difficult to compare immigrant participation across states.

The second difficulty emerges from the fact that not all EU countries are at the same stage of the migratory process. Some countries are more concerned with immigration as such, i.e. with the recent arrival and settlement of migrants, while other countries have already faced several waves of immigration in the past decades and are therefore simultaneously in a migration situation and a post-migration situation. In the former countries issues linked to political participation of migrants are not yet high on the political and academic agenda. In the latter countries, political mobilisation, participation and representation of ethnic migrant minorities have become topical issues. Nevertheless, some of the new EU Member States in Central and Eastern Europe have already introduced a local franchise for all foreign residents, not so much in response to immigrant mobilisations for political representation but in response to EU accession and the provisions of the Maastricht Treaty. Among the Mediterranean states, the Italian parliament passed a law for local voting rights that was eventually blocked for constitutional reasons, while Spain and Portugal have introduced such rights on a basis of reciprocity (see table 2 in the annex).

A third difficulty refers to the fact that 'immigrants and their offspring' are not a homogeneous group in terms of political attitude and behaviour. Some migrants are highly politicised and were politically active in their country of origin from which they often escaped precisely for political reasons. Others, like many native citizens nowadays, are not interested in politics at all.

To be complete, one should also add a technical difficulty related to the unequal availability of adequate statistical data in the various Member States of the EU. For comprehensive statistical analyses one would need data not only on foreign nationality but also on country of birth, on the year of immigration and on ethnic self-identification. It is very difficult to quantify the political behaviour of immigrants and ethnic minorities in countries where only foreign nationality is recorded in official statistics. In other countries, the statistical apparatus is much more developed and data, for example, on ethnic minorities' voting behaviour are easier to produce.

This said, we can still suggest several indicators of political participation of immigrants and their offspring based on a distinction between conventional and less conventional forms of political participation.

When using these indicators, one has to bear in mind that the forms of immigrants' political participation primarily depend on the structure of political opportunities present at a given time and in a given society, which is the result of inclusion-exclusion mechanisms developed by the states (of residence and of origin) and their political systems.

Text Box 10: Anja Van Heelsum, Research on the civic community perspective in the Netherlands

Putnam's work has stimulated the debate on the positive effect of civic communities on democracy. He took Italy and the United States as examples. A similar mechanism may occur within the Dutch situation: an active civic community seems to have a positive effect on political participation within a multicultural democracy. The relationship between different forms of political activity and civic participation in organisations of ethnic minorities in the Netherlands has been the subject of a large number of publications within IMES (e.g. Fennema & Tillie 2001, Van Heelsum 2002, Tillie 2004). The theoretical notions of civic community theories can be used to explain differences between ethnic groups. Turnout rates at elections and the networks of organisations of ethnic minorities throughout the Netherlands show an interesting relationship. Ethnic groups with a high participation rate in elections – like Turks – also tend to have a densely organised network of associations. While ethnic groups with low turnout rates in elections, tend to have fewer associations and a less dense network between their associations. The relationship seems to be mediated by political trust. A community with many associations develops political trust which in turn increases participation.

Indicators of conventional political participation

In the field of conventional political participation, at least five indicators of political participation of immigrants and their offspring can be suggested:
a) Where immigrants and their offspring are enfranchised, how to characterise their electoral turnout as compared to non-immigrant citizens? Do they take part in elections as voters more or less than other citizens? A high electoral turnout can be considered as a good indicator of political participation.
b) Statistical representation of immigrants and their offspring on electoral lists and in elected positions, not to mention in executive branches of government and cabinets in the various assemblies (from the local to the European level) is another indicator of political participation.

c) The rate of membership in political parties and the activity within those parties should also be taken into account as a possible indicator of political participation.
d) In some countries and regions, immigrants and their offspring form their own political parties based on religious or ethnic agendas and run for elections. This form of political behaviour should not be excluded in the process of selecting indicators.
e) Some states, regions or cities have created specific consultative institutions at the margin of the political system to deal specifically with ethnic and immigration issues. There are several hundreds of such consultative bodies across Europe. Participation in these institutions can be seen as an indicator of political participation but it can also be interpreted as a sign of political marginalisation.

Indicators of non-conventional political participation

In the field of non-conventional political participation, we can list at least three indicators of political participation of immigrants and their offspring:
a) The presence of immigrants in trade unions is an old and well-known phenomenon in European countries of immigration. Being active in a trade union either simply as a supporter and member or also as an activist or executive is a relevant indicator of political participation.
b) In order to promote and defend political interests and to exert some pressure on the political system, immigrants and their offspring can organise a collective actor along ethnic, racial, national, cultural or religious lines. This refers, for example, to different types of associations. Here again, the existence of claims-making immigrant associations can be considered as an indicator for participation in the larger political community.
c) Immigrants can also get involved, as any other citizens, in all kinds of pressure groups and movements defending a great variety of interests. Let us mention here humanitarian movements, environmentalist movements, neighbourhood committees, customers' associations, etc. The presence and participation of immigrants in these movements is another indicator of their political participation.

The above list of possible indicators of political participation is far from being exhaustive. It nevertheless points at very relevant forms of political involvement in a democratic society.

A final word of caution: political participation of immigrants and their offspring must always be compared to political participation of non-immigrant citizens prior to pan-European comparison.

Annex

Table 1: Harald Waldrauch, Acquisition of nationality at birth and by naturalisation in Western Europe (15 old EU Member States, Norway and Switzerland)

Country	regular naturalization			ius soli			acquisition after marriage with a citizen	
	minimum residence	toleration of dual nationality	entitlement	at birth for 2nd or 3rd generation	ius soli entitlement[a] after birth for 2nd generation		minimum residence	minimum duration of marriage
Austria	10 years, 4 years for EU/EEA citizens	no	after 30 years	no	no		1, 2 or 5 years residence	1, 2 or 5 years marriage and 4, 3 or 0 years residence
Belgium	3 years	yes	after 7 years (declaration)	3rd gen. if registered by a parent who lived in Belgium for 5 out of 10 years before birth	10 years residence of both parents, registration until age 12		3 years	6 months
Denmark	9 years, 2 years for Nordic citizens	no	for Nordic citizens after 7 years (declaration)	no	no		6-8 years residence and 1-3 years marriage	
Finland	6 years	yes	no	no	no		4 years	3 years
France	5 years	yes	no	automatic for 3rd gen.	5 years residence after age 11: declaration until age 18 or automatic at age 18		1 year residence and 2 years marriage or 3 years marriage if less than 1 year residence	

ANNEX

Country	regular naturalization			ius soli			acquisition after marriage with a citizen	
	minimum residence	toleration of dual nationality	entitlement	at birth for 2nd or 3rd generation	ius soli entitlement[a] after birth for 2nd generation		minimum residence	minimum duration of marriage
Germany	8 years	no; but many exemptions	yes	2nd gen. if a parent has permanent residence title and 8 years of residence[b]	no		3 years	2 years
Greece	10 years	renunciation required in actual practice	no	no	no		3 years if child with one Greek national parent	–
Ireland	4 years	yes	no	2nd gen. if one parent was resident for at least 3 years	yes		2 years	3 years
Italy	10 years, 4 years for EU/EEA citizens	yes	no	no	continuous residence since birth: declaration at age 18		6 months residence or 3 years marriage	
Luxembourg	10 years	no	no	no	5 years: option after age 18		3 years	3 years
Netherlands	5 years	no but many exemptions	unclear	3rd gen.	continuous residence since birth: declaration between age 18-25		no minimum residence and 3 years marriage (naturalisation) or 15 years residence and 3 years marriage (declaration)	

Country	regular naturalization		ius soli		acquisition after marriage with a citizen	
	minimum residence	toleration of dual nationality	entitlement at birth for 2nd or 3rd generation	ius soli entitlement[a] after birth for 2nd generation	minimum residence	minimum duration of marriage
Norway	7 years, shorter for Nordic citizens	no	no	no	7 years minimum residence (may be shortened)	?
Portugal	10 years, 6 years for citizens of lusophone countries	yes	no	2nd gen. if parent resident since 10 years (6 years for citizens of lusophone countries)	no minimum residence	3 years
Spain	10 years, 2 years for citizens of Portugal and some Hispanic states	no, except citizens of Portugal and some Hispanic states	yes	automatic for 3rd gen.	1 year residence	1 year
Sweden	5 years, 2 years for Nordic citizens	yes	no	no	3 years residence and permanent residence title	2 years
Switzerland[c]	12 years	yes	no	no	5 years residence und 3 years marriage, or 6 years residence und close ties to Switzerland	

ANNEX

Country	regular naturalization			ius soli		acquisition after marriage with a citizen	
	minimum residence	toleration of dual nationality	entitlement	at birth for 2nd or 3rd generation	ius soli entitlement[a] after birth for 2nd generation	minimum residence	minimum duration of marriage
UK	5 years	yes	no	2nd gen. if a parent is a permanent resident	if a parent acquires permanent residence or continuous residence since birth until age 10: registration until age 18	3 years	no minimum duration

Comments:
a) 'Ius soli entitlement' refers here only to birth in the territory as a relevant ground for citizenship acquisition after birth. Several states have special provisions for acquisition by minors who have not been born in the territory but have lived there for a certain time. These have not been included in the table. For example, in Sweden foreign nationals who have lived there since age 13 are entitled to claim Swedish citizenship at age 18. In several other countries there are provisions for facilitated naturalisation rather than acquisition by declaration.
b) Dual nationals by birth must choose one nationality between age 18 and 23.
c) The Irish ius soli regime was changed as a result of a referendum in June 2004. The new rule described in this table will come into effect in January 2005.

Sources: data collected by Harald Waldrauch, European Centre for Social Welfare Policy and Research, Vienna (last update: December 2004). Aleinikoff & Klusmeyer 2000, 2001, Davy 2001, Wanner & D'Amato 2003, Hansen & Weil 2002a, Münz & Ulrich 2003, Waldrauch 2001, Weil 2001, Schweizerischer Bundesrat 2001, various websites, information collected by project partners during the EU research project 'The acquisition of nationality in EU Member states: rules, practices and quantitative developments (NATAC)'.

Table 2: Harald Waldrauch, Voting rights of third country nationals in Western Europe (25 EU states, Norway and Switzerland)

	local level		regional level[a]		national level	
	right to vote	eligibility	right to vote	eligibility	right to vote	eligibility
Austria	no		no		no	
Belgium	after 5 years	no	no		no	
Cyprus	no (under discussion)		?		no	
Czech Republic	nationals of countries to which electoral rights have been granted in international treaty (currently no such treaty with non-EU country)		no		no	
Denmark	after 3 years, no minimum residence for Nordic citizens				no	
Estonia	permanent residents (min. residence for PR permit: 3 years) with 5 years residence in municipality	no	no		no	
Germany	no		no		no	
Finland	after 2 years, no minimum residence for Nordic citizens		–		no	
France	no		no		no	
Greece	no		–		no	
Hungary	yes, no minimum residence	no	yes, no minimum residence	no	no	

ANNEX

	local level		regional level[a]		national level	
	right to vote	eligibility	right to vote	eligibility	right to vote	eligibility
Ireland	yes, no minimum residence		–		Parliament (Dáil): British citizens only, no minimum residence President: no	no
Italy	no		no		no	
Latvia	no		–		no	
Lithuania	permanent residents (min. residence for PR permit: 5 years)		–		no	
Luxembourg	after 5 years		–		no	
Malta	nationals of Council of Europe states under condition of reciprocity (currently applies to no non-EU-state) after 6 months residence		–		no	
Netherlands	after 5 years		no		no	
Norway	after 3 years				no	
Poland	No (under discussion)		no		no	
Portugal	nationals of countries with reciprocity agreements after 2–3 years[b]	nationals of countries with reciprocity agreements after 4-5 years[c]	Brazilian nationals with special status after 2 years	no	Brazilian nationals with special status after 2 years	no
Slovakia	permanent residents (min. residence for PR permit: 3 years)					

	local level		regional level[a]		national level	
	right to vote	eligibility	right to vote	eligibility	right to vote	eligibility
Slovenia	permanent residents (min. residence for PR permit: 8 years) but cannot be elected mayor		–		no	
Spain	Norwegian nationals after 3 years		no		no	
Sweden	after 3 years, no minimum residence for Nordic citizens					
Switzerland	after 5-10 years residence in 4 cantons; right can be granted in 2 more cantons[d]	after 5-10 years residence in 3 cantons; right can be granted in 1 more canton[e]	Jura: after 10 years residence in canton; Neuchatel: permanent residents after 5 years residence in canton	no	no	
UK	Commonwealth and Irish citizens, no minimum residence requirements					

Comments:

a) Regional elections in Denmark, Hungary, Norway, Slovakia and Sweden are aspects of local self-government; the franchise is the same as in local elections.
b) Nationals of Brazil and Cape Verde after 2 years, of Argentina, Chile, Israel, Norway, Peru, Uruguay and Venezuela after 3 years.
c) Nationals of Brazil and Cape Verde after 4 years, of Peru and Uruguay after 5 years.
d) Canton Jura: after 10 years residence in canton; canton Neuchatel: permanent residence permit (minimum residence for PR permit: 5-10 years) and 1 year residence in municipality; canton Waadt: after 10 years residence in Switzerland and 3 years in canton; canton Freiburg: after 5 years residence in canton; canton Appenzell-Ausserrhoden: municipalities can grant right to vote after 10 years residence in Switzerland and 5 years in canton (currently in 2 municipalities); Graubünden: municipalities can grant right to vote and be elected.
e) Cantons Jura, Waadt, Freiburg and Graubünden: see above.

Source: data collected by Harald Waldrauch, European Centre for Social Welfare Policy and Research, Vienna (last update: December 2004).

Notes

Introduction

1 We invited two top experts from outside the IMISCOE network to the Vienna workshop, Gerard-René de Groot (Maastricht University), who discussed recent developments in legislation on nationality in Europe, and Kees Groenendijk (Nijmegen University), who analysed European policy making on the status of third country nationals.
2 However, see Brubaker (2001) who analyses recent discourses on assimilation in which the concept is interpreted in a way that closely resembles the use of integration in this report.

Chapter 1

1 For recent overviews see Faulks (2000) and Heater (1999, 2004).
2 See also Shachar (2003) who argues that birthright citizenship is an unjust institution that sustains global inequality.
3 Some states distinguish between citizenship and nationality as two different legal statuses. For example, Mexican expatriates who live permanently abroad are called nationals rather than citizens. The former enjoy rights of diplomatic protection, return to Mexico and land ownership there, but had not possessed the voting rights of Mexican citizens until a law extended the franchise to them in June 2005.
4 Along similar lines, Glick Schiller (2003) and Glick Schiller and Levitt (2004) distinguish between transnational ways of belonging and ways of being, with the latter referring to actual social relations and practices rather than to identities associated with these.
5 Building on Tiebout (1956), Frey & Eichenberger (1999) have used a similar approach to argue for functional, overlapping and competing jurisdictions in which the economic rationale of club membership would be counterbalanced by direct democracy.
6 A club model of citizenship suggests the opposite question: Why do only immigrants have to naturalise? If the political community is a voluntary association, then not only immigrants should naturalise but all native-born citizens should also be asked at the age of majority whether they want to join. Such a conception of voluntary citizenship has been occasionally advocated by libertarian theorists. Many people could then choose to remain stateless or to opt for the citizenship of an external state with which they are not connected through ties and stakes. Instead of defining common rights and duties for the members of a territorial jurisdiction, citizenship would become a strongly differentiated and deterritorialised status and would thus be deprived of its inclusive and egalitarian ethos. Jordan & Düvell (2003) suggest that economic

globalisation may result in a partial deterritorialisation, not of citizenship itself but of certain rights. Non-territorial and globally operating clubs could substitute certain elements of 'social citizenship' by providing health care and higher education to members who can afford to pay.

7   Control over naturalisations by lower-level units within a polity is also characteristic for Switzerland where citizenship of the federation is formally derived from cantonal and municipal citizenship and where naturalisation requirements are defined differently in the various cantons.

8   In the US some of the initial decisions in the 1996 welfare reform that deprived permanent residents of federal welfare benefits were subsequently reversed or compensated by state-based welfare.

9   This claim is broadly supported by historical research on migration, e.g. Hoerder (2002) and Moch (1992).

Chapter 2

1   Mobility rights enjoyed by EU nationals, and by extension, by citizens of the European Economic Area and Switzerland are conceptually different from those of third country nationals. Their status can be interpreted as preferential treatment of nationals of certain countries that is common in many states beyond the European context. From 2005, the implementation of the directive on the status of long term residents (Directive EC (2003) 109) will approximate their mobility rights to those of Union citizens (see chapter 3).

2   For an analysis of regularisation programmes across Europe see De Bruycker, Schmitter & de Seze (2000). Note that de facto refugees in many third world countries are kept in a similarly precarious legal position, irrespective of the length of their stay (Holborn 1975, Kibreab 2003).

3   The 1991 Immigration Law in Greece, for example, introduced permanent residence permits. However, these have been granted only in exceptional cases and have remained largely irrelevant for the bulk of the immigrant population. This is due to the facts that the country has become a major immigrant receiving state only recently and that it imposes an extremely long waiting period (fifteen years of continuous possession of a short-term permit) and in addition demands at least ten years of employment for which social security contributions have been paid.

4   See Jandl, Kraler & Stepien 2003 for brief references to the discriminatory effects of immigration legislation.

5   There are few data on this group. However, it seems plausible to assume that a considerable number of seasonal workers do not return upon termination of their contract, especially if hired for another term. This may frequently be the case in employment that is only affected by seasonal fluctuations in demand, but not necessarily limited to specific times of the year (e.g. construction, tourism), or in other types of short-term employment. Overstaying may be facilitated by the fact that work permits for seasonal employment can often also be obtained from within the country. Data collected in the course of the regularisation programme initiated by the 1986 Immigration Reform and Control Act in the US, however, suggests that seasonal workers in agriculture were indeed the main source of irregular migration to the US (see Meissner 2004, Papademetriou 2004).

6   A similar discrepancy may also be important in the case of other rights theoretically enjoyed after a certain period of residence or employment in certain countries (e.g. right to family reunion, non-restricted or unlimited work permits etc.).

7 Regularisation programmes usually aim at 'capturing' the undocumented immigrant population and thus at reasserting state control, even though they may enhance access to rights, notably residence, employment and social security rights. The new German Immigration Law of 30 July 2004 is one of the few instances where legislators recognised and responded to the problem associated with keeping irregular but documented migrants in a precarious legal status for too long. Thus, albeit the practice of 'toleration' (Duldung) – the status given to in principle removable aliens whose expulsion/ deportation can temporarily not be enforced – continues, 'chain toleration' (Kettenduldung) – i.e. successive periods of toleration – is now effectively prohibited. Henceforth, authorities may grant a residence permit, if the period during which the deportation order cannot be enforced is likely to exceed six months. If an alien has had a 'toleration' status for eighteen months, a residence permit shall be regularly granted. After seven years of residence, the alien may be granted a permanent residence permit (see Art. 24 (5) Immigration Law).

8 Kondo's survey of immigration and citizenship regulations in ten 'western' countries (2001) includes classical immigration countries alongside European immigration countries and Japan, but does not reflect on the different positions of permanent residence within national immigration regimes.

9 A much stronger bias works against the developing world, in particular the developing countries in Africa and Asia. Outside small circles of area specialists, immigration policies of Asian or African countries hardly ever draw the attention of mainstream migration scholars. If one takes the status of labour migrants in the Gulf countries or major African receiving countries (e.g. Nigeria, Libya and Gabon, for all of which some scholarly work exists) as representative for non-European developing countries in general, it seems that there is a general trend to regard the presence of 'outsiders' as temporary and passing and, as a corollary, to discourage their 'integration'. This is reflected both in legal regulations and perhaps more important, by state practice. By and large, refugees are also treated as 'temporary guests', no matter how long the duration of their stay.

10 For example, the Czech Republic's citizenship law of 1993 grants citizenship to all those who have maintained permanent residence in the country for five years (two years for Slovaks) and have had no criminal record for five years. Compared with the residency requirements of other new Member States, such as Latvia and Estonia, which have been intent on denying citizenship to ethnic Russians, the Czech case may seem relatively liberal. In practice, however, Czech citizenship legislation was far from ethnically blind. Permanent legal residence required that an individual be registered with the local authorities – and one third of the Roma population in 1993 were not. Due to this fact 100,000 Roma – about one third of their population in the country – lost their citizenship, and nearly 50 percent of those rendered stateless had lived in the country since birth (Neier 1995).

11 The British Home Office's attempts to denaturalise the radical Muslim cleric Abu Hamza al-Masri, and to eventually expell him, is perhaps indicative of a major change of attitude. The British Home Office had Ali Hamza's British citizenship revoked in April 2003 under a provision of the Nationality, Immigration and Asylum Act 2002 that allows people with dual nationality to be stripped of British citizenship if they act in a way that is judged 'seriously prejudicial' to Britain's 'vital interests' (quoted in the Independent, 7 April 2003). Mr. Hamza appealed against the Home Office's decision arguing that he was no dual citizen and thus would be rendered stateless, were British nationality to be revoked. The British Home Office argued that as a person born in Egypt, Abu Hamza is entitled to Egyptian nationality and thus can be considered a dual national in the meaning of the Nationality, Immigration and Asylum Act. The case is still under review.

12   The following section is largely based on a contribution by Gianni D'Amato.
13   In some states 'special services' to the state, such as military service, may create an entitlement to citizenship. In Austria, for example, foreign university professors automatically acquire Austrian citizenship.
14   Until the early nineteenth century the drafting of soldiers by European powers in the US territories was a major source of conflict over citizenship.
15   Demotic conceptions of citizenship based on co-residence and subjection to a common authority can be contrasted with ethnic conceptions of nationhood.
16   In general, studies of the implementation of citizenship policies by the competent lower level authorities are few and far between. Especially in states that allow for considerable administrative discretion, the official state policy as reflected in citizenship laws may mean little in practice. A particularly fascinating issue is the de facto toleration of dual citizenship by administrative fiat (see also the section on dual citizenship below).
17   In Austria, for example, the proportion of persons naturalised by way of extension grew from over 39.2 per cent in 1991 to 49.6 per cent in 2001.
18   This was not always the case, and signs of allegiance to another country (in particular military service) were traditionally a universally accepted condition for which nationality could be forefeited (Faist, Gerdes & Rieple 2004).
19   Possible sources of conflicts are tax obligations and welfare contributions or benefits in the case of tax-based welfare systems. As most tax obligations are in fact based on residence rather than citizenship, in reality few conflicts occur over the former. Some states, however, notably the US, fully tax their citizens' income earned abroad. Rights and obligations of citizens abroad in the case of tax-based welfare systems are arguably a bigger problem. However, even in this case most entitlements are complemented by residence requirements. Little empirical research exists on possible practical problems arising from dual nationality.
20   States, however, could of course argue that the person who is expatriated because she or he obtained citizenship fraudulently, legally never acquired citizenship.
21   It could be argued that in such a case, and particularly if the state in question is a signatory to the Convention of the Reduction of Statelessness of 30 August 1961, nationality was technically never lost if other states continue to recognise the person's rights to citizenship. While a regime change may lead new democratic elites to publicly regret cases of denaturalisation carried out by a preceding authoritarian regime, whether they annul expatriations or facilitate the reacquisition of citizenship is an altogether different question. As Kolonivits, Burger & Wendelin (2004) demonstrate in their case study of former Austrian citizens (largely Jews), deprived of their nationality during the Nazi regime, Austrian post-war citizenship policy effectively discouraged former citizens from reacquiring Austrian citizenship. Not only were no attempts made to annul withdrawals of citizenship by law, but also the conditions for reacquisition presented major obstacles for a the great majority of in principle eligible persons. Most importantly, dual nationality was not accepted and applicants wishing to reacquire Austrian citizenship had to formally renounce a foreign nationality obtained while in exile. In addition, the reacquisition of citizenship was only granted if applicants established a 'place of residence' in Austria. At the same time, non-nationals were excluded from receiving compensation from public funds established for victims of Nazism after the war, thus – in connection with citizenship laws – creating considerable hardship. It was only in 1993, that the citizenship requirement for beneficiaries of public funds was dropped and dual nationality formally accepted in case of former Austrian citizens deprived of their nationality between 1938 and 1945.

22 A good example for highly inconsistent citizenship legislation and administrative practices as well as for the resulting confusion is the case of the Democratic Republic of Congo, where the large Rwandan minority in the country's eastern Kivu region has been a frequent target of citizenship reforms. The regulations for citizenship have been reformed three times, at one time granting all Rwandans, except post-colonial refugees and migrants who had immigrated just prior to independence, Zairian citizenship, only to withdraw it again in a later reform. The corrupt nature of the Mobutu state, however, meant that most Rwandans were actually able to 'buy' identity cards, while this did not necessarily protect them from expulsion and other forms of harassment directed against them as 'aliens' (see Deng 2001).

23 In many post-communist countries, returned exiles have played an important role during the transition and continue to play an important role in contemporary politics. In turn, they often have an acute interest in maintaining and cultivating ties to exiles who remain abroad. Cape Verde is a particularly interesting case, as the number of Cape Verdians abroad equals that of the resident population. Hence, Cape Verdians abroad, especially those in the US play an important part in politics, and in particular also with respect to citizenship policy and the cultural discourse over 'Cape Verdianness' (Pedro Gois, personal communication).

24 Based on a contribution by Philippe Wanner (SFM).

25 The Swiss census, however, includes a question on the date when citizenship was acquired, with 'since birth' or the specific year being the two options. In addition, the Swiss census also includes a question on dual nationality.

26 The German Socio-Economic Panel may be cited as an example for such a survey.

27 The following section follows an argument developed in Waldrauch and Çinar (2003).

28 Narrowly interpreted, naturalisation rates are demographic indicators and measure the decline of the foreign resident population by way of naturalisation.

29 Arguably, the low naturalisation propensity of EU citizens who are resident in another Member State may be attributed to the limited additional rights a Member States' citizenship confers.

30 See Fink-Nielsen, Hansen & Kleist 2004 for evidence that migrants may choose a western citizenship if they intend to return to their countries of origin. See also Kibreab (2003) for a more general argument.

31 See Scott 2004 and Bevelander & Veenmann 2004 for European case studies based on relatively comprehensive data. Kogan's (2003) comparative analysis of the consequences of naturalisation for Ex-Yugoslavs in Austria and Sweden shows that research on the 'economics of citizenship' can to a certain extent also be done on the basis of more limited data.

Chapter 3

1 Before the introduction of Union citizenship, the term 'foreigner' was used in EC-documents to denote citizens of Member States living in another Member State. The usage here refers to this understanding.

2 Rudy Grzelczyk vs. Centre public d'aide sociale d'Ottignies-Louvain-la-Neuve, C-184-99, 20 September 2001.

3 Michelleti vs. Delegacion del Gobierno en Cantabria (1992), ECR - I 4239.

4 Declaration No 2 on nationality of a Member State appended to the Maastricht Treaty confirms that the question of whether an individual possesses the nationality of a Member State is settled solely by reference to the national law of the Member State concerned. Access to Union citizenship is thus defined through national laws on nationality, including conditions for naturalisation.

5 European Parliament and Council Directive 2004/38/EC on the right of citizens of the Union and their family members to move and reside freely within the territory of the Member States, amending Regulation (EEC) No 1612/68 and repealing Directives 64/221/EEC, 68/360/EEC, 72/194/EEC, 73/148/EEC,75/34/EEC, 75/35/EEC, 90/365/EEC, 90/365/EEC and 93/96/EEC, Official Journal (OJ) L 158, 30 April 2004, p. 77.
6 Germany and others vs. Commission (1987) ECR, I-3254; see also Hoogenboom (1992: 39).
7 Agreement Establishing an Association between the EEC and Turkey, signed at Ankara, 12 September 1963, approved on behalf of the Community by Council Decision 64/732/EEC of 23 December 1963 (OJ 1973 C 113), Decision of the Association Council No. 2/76 on the implementation of Article 12 of the Ankara Agreement (adopted at the 23rd meeting of the Association Council on 20 December 1976), Decision No 1/80 of the Association Council of 19 September 1980 on the development of the Association, Decision No 3/80 of the Association Council of 19 September 1980 on the application of the social security schemes of the Member States of the European Communities to Turkish workers and members of their families. As both decisions never have been published in the OJ, the court first had to decide on their legal status. In the case Meryem Demirel vs. Stadt Schwäbisch Gmünd (case 12/86), it declared that the Decisions of the Association Council formed a part of the acquis communautaire.
8 Ömer Nazl et al. vs. Stadt Nürnberg (C-340/97) (2000) ECR I-957.
9 Engin Ayaz vs. Land Baden-Würtemberg, C-275/02, 30 September 2004.
10 Ahmet Bozkurt vs. Staatssecretaris van Justitie (C-434/93) (1995) ECR I-1475.
11 Proposal for a Council Directive concerning the status of third country nationals who are long-term residents, COM (2001) 127 final, Proposal for a Council Directive on conditions of entry and residence for third country nationals for the purpose of paid employment and self employed economic activity, Proposal for a Council Directive on the right to family reunification, (COM (1999) 638 final.
12 Council Directive 2003/109/EC of 25 November 2003 concerning the status of third country nationals who are long-term residents, OJ L 016, 23 January 2004; Council Directive 2003/86/EC of 22 September 2003 on the right to family reunification, OJ L 251, 3 October 2003, pp. 0012-0018.
13 See footnote 1 of this chapter.
14 Council Directive 2003/109/EC of 25 November 2003 concerning the status of third country nationals who are long-term residents.
15 Council Directive 2000/43/EC of 29 June 2000 implementing the principle of equal treatment between persons irrespective of racial or ethnic origin.
16 Council Directive 2000/78/EC of 27 November 2000 establishing a general framework for equal treatment in employment and occupation.
17 For a critical evaluation see Bauböck (2004b).

Chapter 4

1 Using a social capital approach, Fennema and Tillie have argued that dense associational networks within ethnic groups enhance political trust and participation (Fennema & Tillie 2001, 2004; Jacobs & Tillie 2004; Heelsum 2004).
2 The United Kingdom is exceptional in this regard since it extends active voting rights as well as eligibility in national elections to all Commonwealth and Irish citizens.
3 An ethnic block vote in this second sense includes also ethnic group patterns in voting in referenda and plebiscites.

References

Alba, R. & V. Nee (2003), *Remaking the American Mainstream. Assimilation and Contemporary Immigration*. Cambridge, MA: Harvard University Press.
Al-Bustānī, S. Y. (2003), *al-ǧinsiyya wa 'l-qawmiyya fī tašrīʿāt al-duwal al-ʿarabiyya.Dirāsat muqārana*. Beyrūt: Manšūrāt al-Halabī al-qānūniyya.
Aleinikoff, A. T. (2000), 'Between Principles and Policies: U.S. Citizenship Policy', in A. T. Aleinikoff & D. Klusmeyer (eds.), *From Migrants to Citizens. Membership in a Changing World*, 119-174. Washington, DC: Carnegie Endowment for International Peace.
Aleinikoff, A. T. & D. Klusmeyer (eds.) (2000), *From Migrants to Citizens. Membership in a Changing World*. Washington, DC: Carnegie Endowment for Peace.
Aleinikoff, A. T. & D. Klusmeyer (eds.) (2001), *Citizenship today: Global Perspectives and Practices*. Washington, DC: Carnegie Endowment for International Peace.
Aleinikoff, A. T. & D. Klusmeyer (eds.) (2002), *Citizenship Policies for an Age of Migration*. Washington, DC: Carnegie Endowment for International Peace.
Apap, J. & S. Carrera (2003), 'Towards a Proactive Immigration Policy for the EU?', *CEPS Working Document* 198. www.ceps.be.
Bader, V. (1997), 'Differentiated Egalitarian Multiculturalism', in R. Bauböck (ed.) *Blurred Boundaries. Migration, Ethnicity, Citizenship*, 185-220. Aldershot: Ashgate.
Bader, V. (2001), 'Institutions, Culture and Identity of Trans-National Citizenship: How much Integration and "Communal Spirit" is needed?', in: C. Crouch & K. Eder (eds.), *Citizenship, Markets, and the State*, 192-212. Oxford: Oxford University Press.
Barrington, L. W. (2000), 'Understanding citizenship in the Baltic States', in A. T. Aleinikoff & D. Klusmeyer (eds.), *From Migrants to Citizens. Membership in a Changing World*, 253-301. Washington DC: Carnegie Endowment for International Peace.
Bauböck, R. (1994), *Transnational Citizenship. Membership and Rights in International Migration*. Aldershot: Edward Elgar.
Bauböck, R. (2002), 'Farewell to Multiculturalism? Sharing values and identities in societies of immigration', *Journal of International Migration and Integration* 3 (1): 1-16.
Bauböck, R. (2003a), 'Towards a political theory of migrant transnationalism', *International Migration Review* 37 (3): 700-723.
Bauböck, R. (2003b), 'Public culture in societies of immigration', in R. Sackmann, T. Faist & B. Peters (eds.), *Identity and Integration. Migrants in Western Europe*, 37-57. Aldershot: Ashgate.
Bauböck, R. (2004a), 'Citizenship Policies: International, state, migrant and democratic perspectives', *Global Migration Perspectives* 19. www.gcim.org.
Bauböck, R. (2004b), 'Civic Citizenship – A New Concept for the New Europe', in R. Süssmuth & W. Weidenfeld (eds.), *Managing Integration. The European Union's Responsibilities towards Immigrants*. Gütersloh: Bertelsmann Stiftung.
Belkeziz, A. (1963), *La nationalité dans les États arabes*. Rabat: La Porte.
Bell, M. (2002a), *Anti-Discrimination Law and the European Union*. New York: Oxford University Press.
Bell, M. (2002b), 'Combating racism through European laws: a comparison of the Racial Equality Directive and Protocol 12', in I. Chopin & J. Niessen (eds.), *Combating Racial*

and Ethnic Discrimination. Taking the European Legislative Agenda further, 7-34. London etc.: Commission for Racial Equality etc. www.migpolgroup.com.

Benedikt, C. (2004), *Diskursive Konstruktion Europas. Migration und Entwicklungspolitik im Prozess der Europäisierung*. Frankfurt/Main: Brandes & Apsel.

Bevelander, P. & J. Veenmann (2004), 'Naturalization and Immigrants' Employment Integration in the Netherlands', paper presented at the conference 'Immigrant ascension to citizenship: recent policies and economic and social consequences', International conference organised under the auspices of the Willy Brandt Guest Professorship's Chair International Migration and Ethnic Relations (IMER), Malmö University, 7 June 2004.

Boswell, C. (2003), 'The "external dimension" of EU immigration and asylum policy', *International Affairs* 79 (3): 619-638.

Bousetta, H. & M. Martiniello (2003), 'L'immigration marocaine en Belgique : du travailleur immigré au citoyen transnational', *Hommes et Migrations* 1242: 94-106.

Bratsberg B., J. F. Ragan & Z. M. Nasir (2002), 'The Effect of Naturalization on Wage Growth', *Journal of Labor Economics* 22 (3): 568-597.

British Council (2005), *European Civic Citizenship and Inclusion Index*. British Council Brussels: Foreign Policy Centre and Migration Policy Group. www.britishcouncil.org/brussels-europe-inclusion-index.htm.

Brubaker, R. (ed.) (1989), *Immigration and the Politics of Citizenship in Europe and North America*. New York: University Press of America and German Marshall Fund of the United States.

Brubaker, R. (1992), *Citizenship and Nationhood in France and Germany*. Cambridge: Harvard University Press.

Brubaker, R. (1994), 'Nationhood and the National Question in the Soviet Union and Post-Soviet Union Eurasia: An Institutionalist Account', *Theory and Society* 23 (1): 47-78.

Brubaker, R. (2001), 'The Return of Assimilation', *Ethnic and Racial Studies* 24 (4): 531-548.

Buchanan, J. (1965), 'An Economic Theory of Clubs', *Economica* 32: 1-14.

Bultmann, P. F. (2002), 'Dual Nationality and Naturalisation Policies in the German Länder, in R. Hansen & P. Weil (eds.), *Dual Nationality, Social Rights and Federal Citizenship in the U.S. and Europe. The Reinvention of Citizenship*, 136-157. New York etc.: Berghahn Books.

Butenschon, N. A., U. Davis & M. Hassassian (eds.) (2000), *Citizenship and the State in the Middle East: Approaches and Applications*. Syracuse: Syracuse University Press.

Carens, J. H. (1992), 'Migration and Morality. A Liberal Egalitarian Perspective', in B. Barry & R. E. Goodin (eds.), *Free Movement. Ethical Issues in the transnational migration of people and of money*, 25-47. Pennsylvania: The Pennsylvania State University Press.

Castles, S. & A. Davidson (2000), *Citizenship and Migration. Globalization and the Politics of Belonging*. London: Routledge.

CBS (2003), *Allochtonen in Nederland*. Voorburg: CBS.

Cesarani, D. & M. Fulbrook (eds.) (1996), *Citizenship, Nationality and Migration in Europe*. London etc.: Routledge.

Chopin, I. & J. Niessen (eds.) (2001), *The Starting Line and the Incorporation of the Racial Equality Directive into the National Laws of the EU Member States and Accession States*. London etc.: Commission for Racial Equality etc. www.migpolgroup.com.

Chopin, I. & J. Niessen (eds.) (2002), *Combating Racial and Ethnic Discrimination. Taking the European Legislative Agenda further*. London etc.: Commission for Racial Equality etc. www.migpolgroup.com.

Christiansen, F. & U. Hedetoft (eds.) (2004), *The Politics of Multiple Belonging. Ethnicity and Nationalism in Europe and East Asia*. Aldershot: Ashgate.

Cicekli, B. (2003), 'Legal Integration of Turkish Immigrants under the Turkish-EU Association Law', paper presented at the conference 'Integration of immigrants from Turkey in Austria, Germany and Holland', Boğaziçi University, Centre for European Studies, 27 February 2004. www.ces.boun.edu.tr.

Cohen, R. (1997), *Global Diasporas. An Introduction*. London: UCL Press.

Commission of the European Communities (2004), *Report from the Commission. Fourth Report on Citizenship of the Union (1 May 2001-30 April 2004)*. COM (2004) 695 final, 26 October 2004.

Connolly, A., S. Day & J. Shaw (2006), 'The contested case of EU electoral rights', forthcoming in R. Bellamy, D. Castiglione & J. Shaw (eds.), *Making European Citizens: Context*. London: Palgrave. www.law.manchester.ac.uk/staff/jo_shaw.htm.

Council of Europe (1995), *Measurement and indicators of integration*. Strasbourg: Council of Europe.

Dahl, R. A. (1989), *Democracy and its Critics*. New Haven, CT etc.: Yale University Press.

Davy, U. (ed.) (2001), *Die Integration von Einwanderern. Rechtliche Regelungen im europäischen Vergleich*. Frankfurt/Main etc.: Campus.

Day, S. & J. Shaw (2003), 'The Boundaries of Suffrage and External Conditionality. Estonia as an Applicant Member of the EU', *European Public Law* 9 (2): 211-236.

De Bruycker, P., C. Schmitter & S. de Seze (2000), 'Rapport de Synthèse sur la Comparaison des Régularisations d'Étrangers Illégaux dans L'Union Européenne', in P. de Bruycker (ed.), *Les Régularisations des Étrangers Illégaux dans l'Union Européenne*, 24-82. Bruxelles: Bruyant.

De Groot, G.-R. (1989), *Staatsangehörigkeitsrecht im Wandel*. Köln etc.: Heymans.

De Groot, G.-R. (2003), 'Loss of Nationality. A Critical Inventory', in D. A. Martin & K. Hailbronner (eds.), *Rights and Duties of Dual Nationals. Evolution and Prospects*, 201-299. The Hague: Kluwer Law International.

De Groot, G.-R. (2004), 'Towards a European Nationality Law – Vers un droit européen de nationalité', Inaugural lecture delivered on the occasion of the acceptance of the Pierre Harmel chair of professeur invité at the Université de Liège, 13 November 2003. Maastricht: Universiteit Maastricht.

DeVoretz, D. J. & S. Pivnenko (2004), 'The Economics of Canadian Citizenship', *Willy Brandt Series of Working Papers in International Migration and Ethnic Relations* 3. Malmö: Malmö University. www.mah.se.

Delanty, G. (2000), *Citizenship in a global age. Society, culture, politics*. Buckingham etc.: Open University Press.

Deng, F. M. (2001) 'Ethnic Marginalization as Statelessness: Lessons from the Great Lakes Region of Africa', in: A. T. Aleinikoff & D. Klusmeyer (eds.) (2001), *Citizenship Today: Global Perspectives and Practices*, 183-208. Washington, DC: Carnegie Endowment for International Peace.

De Wenden, C. W. (1988), *Les immigrés et la politique*. Paris: Presses de la Fondation Nationale des Sciences Politiques.

De Wenden, C. W. (1999), 'Post-Amsterdam Migration Policy and European Citizenship', *European Journal of Migration and Law* 1: 89-101.

Diehl, C. & M. Blohm (2003), 'Rights or Identity? Naturalization Processes among "Labour Migrants" in Germany', *International Migration Review* 37: 133-161.

Dogan, V. (2002), *Türk Vatandaslik Hukuku*. Ankara: Yetkin Basimevi.

Donner, R. (2004), 'Review of Hansen/Weil 2002 and Martin/Hailbronner 2003', *International and Comparative Law Quarterly* 53 (3): 1041-1045.

Dowty, A. (1987) *Closed Borders. The Contemporary Assault on Freedom of Movement*. New Haven, CT: Yale University Press.

Eder, K. & B. Giessen (2001), *European Citizenship. National Legacies and Transnational Projects*. Oxford: Oxford University Press.
Engelen, E. (2003), 'How to Combine Openness and Protection? Citizenship, Migration and Welfare Regimes', *Politics and Society* 31 (4): 503-536.
Entzinger, H. (2004), *Integration and Orientation Courses in a European Perspective. Expert report written for the Sachverständigenrat für Zuwanderung und Integration*. www.bafl. de/template/zuwanderungsrat/expertisen_2004/expertise_entzinger.pdf.
Eurostat (2002), *The social situation in the European Union 2002*. Luxembourg: Eurostat.
Everson, M. (2003), '"Subjects", or "Citizens of Erwhon"? Law and Non-Law in the Development of a "British Citizenship"', *Citizenship Studies* 7 (1): 57-84.
Faist, T. (2000), *The Volume and Dynamics of International Migration*. New York: Oxford University Press.
Faist, T., J. Gerdes & B. Rieple (2004), 'Dual Citizenship as a Path-Dependent Process', *International Migration Review* 38 (3): 913-944.
Faulks, K. (2000), *Citizenship*. London: Routledge.
Favell, A. (1998), 'Multicultural Race Relations in Britain: Problems of Interpretation and Explanation', in C. Joppke (ed.), *Challenge to the Nation-State. Immigration in Western Europe and the United States*, 319-349. Oxford: Oxford University Press.
Favell, A. (2001), 'Integration policy and integration research in Europe: a review and critique', in A. T. Aleinikoff & D. Klusmeyer (eds.), *Citizenship Today. Global Perspectives and Practices*, 349-399. Washington, DC: Carnegie Endowment for International Peace.
Fennema, M. (2004), 'Concept and Measurement of Civic Communities', *Journal of Ethnic and Migration Studies* 30 (3): 429-447.
Fennema, M. & J. Tillie (2001), 'Civic community, political participation and political trust of ethnic groups', *Connections* 23 (2): 44-59.
Fennema, M. & J. Tillie (forthcoming), 'Social Capital of Migrants', in D. Castiglione, J. van Deth & G. Wolleb (eds.), *Handbook of Social Capital*. Oxford: Oxford University Press.
Fink-Nielsen, M., P. Hansen & N. Kleist (2004), 'Roots, Rights and Responsibilities. Place-making and Repatriation among Somalis in Denmark and Somaliland', *Stichproben. Wiener Zeitschrift für kritische Afrikawissenschaften* 4 (7): 25-47.
Follesdal, A. (2001), 'Union citizenship: Unpacking the beast of burden', in *Law and Philosphy* 20: 313-343.
Freeman, G. P. (1998), 'The Decline of Sovereignty? Politics and Immigration Restriction in Liberal States', in C. Joppke (ed.), *Challenge to the Nation-State. Immigration in Western Europe and the United States*, 86-108. Oxford: Oxford University Press.
Frey, B. & R. Eichenberger (1999), *The New Democratic Federalism for Europe. Functional, Overlapping and Competing Jurisdictions*. Cheltenham: Edward Elgar.
Galbreath, D. J. (2004), 'International Sources of Domestic Policy: Europe and Latvia in the context of minority rights', paper presented at the European Consortium for Political Research joint sessions workshop on 'International Organisations and Policy Implementation', Uppsala Universitet, 13-18 April 2004.
Geddes, A. (1998), 'Race Related Political Participation and Representation in the UK', *Revue Européenne des Migrations Internationales* 14 (2): 33-49.
Geddes, A. & V. Guiraudon (2002), 'Anti-discrimination Policy: The Emergence of a EU Policy Paradigm amidst Contrasted National Models', paper presented at the workshop 'Opening the Black Box: Europeanisation, Discourse, and Policy Change', Oxford, 23-24 November 2002.
Geisser, V. (1997), *Ethnicité Républicaine*. Paris: Presses de Sc.Po.
Ghali, P. (1934), *Les nationalités détachées de l'Empire ottoman à la suite de la Guerre*. Paris : Domat-Montchrestien.

Glick Schiller, N. (2003), 'Transnational Theory and Beyond', in D. Nugent & V. Joan (eds.), *A Companion to the Anthropology of Politics*. Malden, MA: Blackwell.
Glick Schiller, N., N. Basch & C. Blanc-Szanton (1992), *Towards a Transnational Perspective on Migration. Race, Class, Ethnicity and Nationalism Reconsidered*. Annals of the New York Academy of Sciences 645. New York: New York Academy of Sciences.
Glick Schiller, N., N. Basch & C. Blanc-Szanton (1994), *Nations Unbound. Transnational Projects, Postcolonial Predicaments, and Deterritorialized Nation-States*. New York: Routledge.
Glick Schiller, N., N. Basch & C. Blanc-Szanton (1995), 'From Immigrant to Transmigrant: Theorizing Transnational Migration', *Anthropological Quarterly* 68 (1): 48-63.
Glick Schiller, N. & P. Levitt (2004), 'Conceptualizing Simultaneity: A Transnational Social Field Perspective on Society', *International Migration Review* 38 (3): 1002-1039.
Górny, A., A. Grzymała-Kazłowska, P. Koryś & A. Weinar (2006), 'Selective tolerance? Regulations, Practice and Discussions Regarding Dual Nationality in Poland', *International Migration Review* (forthcoming).
Gosewinkel, D. (2001), *Einbürgern und ausschließen. Die Nationalisierung der Staatsangehörigkeit vom Deutschen Bund bis zur Bundesrepublik Deutschland*. Göttingen: Vandenhoek & Ruprecht.
Groenendijk, K., E. Guild & R. Barzilay (2000), *The Legal Status of third country nationals who are long term residents in a Member State of the European Union*. Nijmegen: Centre for Migration Law.
Gsir, S. & M. Martiniello (2004), *Local consultative bodies for foreign residents – a handbook*. Strasbourg: Council of Europe Publishing.
Guarnizo, L. (2003), 'The Economics of Transnational Living', *International Migration Review* 37 (3): 666-699.
Guild, E. (1996), 'The legal framework of citizenship in the European Union, in D. Cesarani & M. Fulbrook (eds.), *Citizenship, Nationality and Migration in Europe*, 30-57. London etc.: Routledge.
Guild, E. (2004), *The emerging Constitution of the European Union: Citizenship, Justice and Security*. Brussels: European Commission, DG EAC – Jean Monnet Project. europa.eu.int/comm/education/programmes/ajm/people_culture/contributions/elspeth_guild_en.pdf.
Guiraudon, V. (1998), 'Citizenship Rights for Non-Citizens: France, Germany, and the Netherlands', in C. Joppke (ed.), *Challenge to the Nation-State. Immigration in Western Europe and the United States*, 272-318. Oxford: Oxford University Press.
Guiraudon, V. (2001): 'The EU "garbage can": Accounting for policy developments in the immigration domain', paper presented at the 2001 conference of the European Community Studies Association, Madison Wisconsin, 29 May-1 June 2001.
Guiraudon, V. (2003), 'The constitution of a European policy domain: a political sociology approach', *Journal of European Public Policy* 10 (2): 263-282.
Guiraudon, V. & G. Lahav (2000), 'A Reappraisal of the State-Sovereignty Debate. The Case of Migration Control', *Comparative Political Studies* 33 (2): 163-195.
Hammar, T. (ed.) (1985), *European immigration policy: a comparative study*. Cambridge: Cambridge University Press.
Hammar, T. (1990), *Democracy and the Nation State. Aliens, Denizens and Citizens in a World of International Migration*. Aldershot: Ashgate.
Hampshire, J. (2005), *Citizenship and Belonging. Immigration and the Politics of Demographic Governance in Post-war Britain*. Basingstoke: Palgrave.
Hansen, R. (2000), *Citizenship and immigration in post-war Britain*. Oxford: Oxford University Press.
Hansen, R. (2002), 'Globalization, Embedded Realism, and Path Dependance. The Other Immigrants to Europe', *Comparative Political Studies* 35 (3): 259-283.

Hansen, R. & P. Weil (eds.) (2001a), *Towards a European Nationality. Citizenship, Immigration and Nationality Law in the EU*. Basingstoke: Palgrave.

Hansen, R. & P. Weil (2001b), 'Introduction: Citizenship, Immigration and Nationality: Towards a Convergence in Europe?', in R. Hansen & P. Weil (eds.), *Towards a European Nationality. Citizenship, Immigration and Nationality Law in the EU*, 1-24. Basingstoke: Palgrave.

Hansen, R. & P. Weil (eds.) (2002a), *Dual Nationality, Social rights and Federal Citizenship in the U.S. and Europe. The Reinvention of Citizenship*. New York etc.: Berghahn Books.

Hansen, R. & P. Weil (2002b), 'Dual Citizenship in A Changed World: Immigration, Gender and Social Rights', in R. Hansen & P. Weil (eds.), *Dual Nationality, Social Rights and Federal Citizenship in the U.S. and Europe. The Reinvention of Citizenship*, 1-15. New York etc.: Berghahn Books.

Heater, D. (1999), *What is Citizenship?* London: Polity Press.

Heater, D. (2004), *A Brief History of Citizenship*. Edinburgh: Edinburgh University Press.

Herbst, J. (2000), *States and Power in Africa. Comparative Lessons in Authority and Control*. Princeton, NJ: Princeton University Press.

Hoerder, D. (2002), *Cultures in Contact: World Migrations in the Second Millennium*. Durham: Duke University Press.

Holborn, L. W. with assistance from P. Chartrand & R. Chartrand (1975), *Refugees: A problem of our time. The work of the United Nations High Commissioner for Refugees. 1951-1972*. Metuchen: Scarecrow Press.

Hoogenboom, T. (1992), 'Integration into Society and the Free Movement of Non-Community Nationals', *European Journal of International Law* 3: 36-54.

Howard, M. (2005), 'Variation in Dual Citizenship Policies in the Countries of the EU', *International Migration Review* 39 (3): 697-720.

Itzigsohn, J. (2000), 'Immigration and the Boundaries of Citizenship: The Institutions of Immigrants' Political Transnationalism', *International Migration Review* 34 (4): 1126-1154.

Jacobson D. (1996), *Rights across Borders. Immigration and the Decline of Citizenship*. Baltimore: Johns Hopkins University Press.

Jandl, M., A. Kraler & A. Stepien (2003), *Migrants, Minorities and Employment: Exclusion, Discrimination and Anti-Discrimination in the 15 Member States of the European Union*. Luxembourg: Office for Official Publications of the European Union. eumc.eu.int/eumc/material/pub/comparativestudy/CS-Employment-en.pdf

Jawhari, R. (2000), *Wegen Überfremdung abgelehnt*. Vienna: Braumüller.

Jellinek, G. (1892), *System der subjektiven öffentlichen Rechte*. Freiburg: Mohr.

Joppke, C. (1998), 'Immigration Challenges the Nation State', in C. Joppke (ed.), *Challenge to the Nation-State. Immigration in Western Europe and the United States*, 5-46. Oxford: Oxford University Press.

Joppke, C. (1999), 'How immigration is changing citizenship: a comparative view', *Ethnic and Racial Studies* 22 (4): 629-692.

Joppke, C. (2001), 'The Legal-Domestic Sources of Immigrant Rights', *Comparative Political Studies* 34 (4): 339-366.

Joppke, C. (2004), 'Citizenship without Identity', *Canadian Diversity/ Diversité Canadienne* 3 (2): 85-87.

Joppke, C. (2005), *Selecting by Origin: Ethnic Migration in the Liberal State*. Cambridge, MA: Harvard University Press.

Jordan, B. & F. Düvell (2003), *Migration. The Boundaries of Equality and Justice*. Cambridge: Polity Press.

Joseph, S. (ed.) (2000), *Gender and Citizenship in the Middle East*. Syracuse: Syracuse University Press.

Kibreab, G. (2003), 'Citizenship Rights and Repatriation of Refugees', *International Migration Review* 37 (1): 24-73.
Kleger, H. (ed.) (1997), *Transnationale Staatsbürgerschaft*. Frankfurt/Main: Campus.
Klusmeyer, D. (2001), 'Introduction', in A. T. Aleinikoff & D. Klusmeyer (eds.), *Citizenship today: Global Perspectives and Practices*. 1-14. Washington, DC: Carnegie Endowment for International Peace.
Kofman, E. (2002), 'Contemporary European migrations, civic stratification and citizenship', *Political Geography* 21: 1035-1054.
Kogan, I. (2003), 'Ex-Yugoslavs in the Austrian and Swedish Labour Markets: The Significance of the Period of Migration and the Effect of the Acquisition of Citizenship', *Journal of Ethnic and Migration Studies* 29 (4): 595-622.
Kolonivits, D., H. Burger & H. Wendelin (2004), *Staatsbürgerschaft und Vertreibung*. Veröffentlichungen der Österreichischen Historikerkommission. Vermögensentzug während der NS-Zeit sowie Rückstellungen und Entschädigungen seit 1945 in Österreich, 7. Vienna: Oldenburg.
Kondo, A. (2001), 'Comparative Citizenship and Aliens' Rights', in A. Kondo (ed.), *Citizenship in a Global World. Comparing Citizenship Rights for Aliens*, 225-250. Houndsmill etc.: Palgrave.
Kostakopoulou, D. (2000), 'The "Protective Union": Change and Continuity in Migration Law and Policy in Post-Amsterdam Europe', *Journal of Common Market Studies* 38 (3): 497-518.
Kostakopoulou, D. (2002), 'Long-term resident third-country nationals in the European Union: normative expectations and institutional openings', *Journal of Ethnic and Migration Studies* 28 (3): 443-462.
Kostakopoulou, D. (2003), 'Why Naturalisation?, *Perspectives on European Politics and Society* 4 (1): 85-115.
Kraler, A., M. Jandl & M. Hofmann (2006), 'The Evolution of EU Migration Policy and Implications for Data Collection', in M. Poulain, N. Perrin & A. Singleton (eds.), *THESIM. Towards Harmonised European Statistics on International Migration*, 35-75. Louvain-la-Neuve: UCL-Presses Universitaires de Louvain.
Kymlicka, W. (1995), *Multicultural Citizenship. A Liberal Theory of Minority Rights*. Oxford: Oxford University Press.
Kymlicka, W. & W. Norman (1994), 'The Return of the Citizen: A Survey of Recent Work on Citizenship Theory', *Ethics* 104: 352-381.
Kymlicka, W. & A. Patten (eds.) (2003), *Language Rights and Political Theory*. Oxford: Oxford University Press.
Lefebvre, E. L. (2003), 'Belgian Citizenship: Managing Linguistic, Regional, and Economic Demands', *Citizenship Studies* 7 (1): 111-134.
Levitt, P. (2001), *The Transnational Villagers*. Berkeley, CA: University of California Press.
Levy, D. & Y. Weiss (eds.) (2002), *Challenging Ethnic Citizenship. German and Israeli Perspectives on Immigration*. Oxford: Berghahn.
Levy, J. (2000), *The Multiculturalism of Fear*. Oxford: Oxford University Press.
Liegl, B., B. Perchinig & B. Weyss (2004), *Combating Ethnic and Religious Discrimination in Employment. From the EU and International Perpective*. Brussels: European Network Against Racism. www.enar-eu.org.
Lockwood, D. (1996), 'Civic Stratification and Class Formation', *The British Journal of Sociology* 47 (3): 531-550.
Mandaville, P. (2001), *Transnational Muslim Politics – Reimagining the Umma*. London: Routledge.
Marshall, T. H. (1965), 'Citizenship and Social Class', in T. H. Marshall, *Class, Citizenship, and Social Development. Essays by T. H. Marshall*. New York: Anchor Books.

Martin, D. A. & K. Hailbronner (eds.) (2003), *Rights and Duties of Dual Nationals: Evolution and Prospects*. The Hague: Kluwer Law International.
Martiniello, M. (1992), *Leadership et pouvoir dans les communautés d'origine immigrée*. Paros: CIEMI, L'Harmattan.
Martiniello, M. (1997), 'Quelle participation politique?', in M.-T. Coenen & R. Lewin (eds.), *La Belgique et ses immigrés – Les politiques manquées*, 101-120. Bruxelles: De Boeck Université.
Martiniello, M. (1998), 'Les immigrés et les minorités ethniques dans les institutions politiques: ethnicisation des systèmes politiques européens ou renforcement de la démocratie?', *Revue Européenne des Migrations Internationales* 14 (2): 9-17.
Meehan, E. (1993), *Citizenship and the European Community*. London: Sage.
Meissner, D. (2004), 'U.S. Temporary Workers Programmes: Lessons Learned', *Migration Information Source*, 1 March 2004. www.migrationinformation.org.
Menz, G. (2002), 'Patterns in EU Labour Immigration Policy. National Initiatives and European Responses', *Journal of Ethnic and Migration Studies* 28 (4): 723-742.
Michalowski, I. (2004), *An Overview on Introduction Programmes in Seven European Member States*. The Hague: Adviescommissie voor Vreedmelingenzaken.
Michon, L. & J. Tillie (2003), *Amsterdamse Polyfonie. Opkomst en stemgedrag van allochtone Amsterdammers bij de gemeenteraads- en deelraadsverkiezingen van 6 maart 2002*. Amsterdam: IMES.
Miller, M. J. (1981), *Foreign Workers in Western Europe. An emerging political force*. New York: Praeger.
Moch, L. P. (1992), *Moving Europeans. Migration in Western Europe since 1650*. Urbana: Indiana University Press.
Morris, L. (2001a), *Managing Migration: Civic Stratification and Migrants' Rights*. London: Routledge.
Morris, L. (2001b), 'The Ambigous Terrain of Rights. Civic Stratification in Italy's Emergent Immigration Regime', *International Journal for Urban and Regional Research* 25 (3): 497-518.
Morris, L. (2003), 'Managing Contradictions: Civic Contradiction: Civic Stratification and Migrants' Rights', *International Migration Review* 37 (1): 74-100.
Münz, R. & R. Ohliger (eds.) (2003), *Diasporas and Ethnic Migrants: Germany, Israel and Post-Soviet Successor States in Comparative Perspective*. London: Frank Cass.
Münz, R. & R. Ulrich (2003), *Das Schweizer Bürgerrecht*. Zürich: Avenir Suisse.
Neier, A. (1995), 'Watching Rights', *Nation* 260 (17)
Nyberg-Sørensen, N. & K. F. Olwig (eds.) (2002), *Work and Migration – Life and Livelihoods in a Globalizing World*. London: Routledge.
Oldfield, A. (1990), *Citizenship and Community. Civic Republicanism and the Modern World*. London: Routledge.
Papademetriou, D. G. (2004), 'The Mexico Factor in Immigration Reform', *Migration Information Source*, 1 March 2004. www.migrationinformation.org.
Parekh, B. (2000), *Rethinking Multiculturalism*. Basingstoke: Macmillan.
Penninx, R. & A. van Heelsum (2004), *Bondgenoot of Spelbreker? Organisaties van immigranten en hun mogelijke rol in integratieprocessen*. Utrecht: FORUM.
Perchinig, B. (2003), 'Effektive Antidiskriminierungspolitik: Ein Produkt konfliktorientierter Sozialmodelle?', *EIF Working Papers* 8. www.eif.oeaw.ac.at.
Però, D. (2002), 'The Left and the Political Participation of Immigrants in Italy: The Case of the Forum of Bologna', in R. Grillo & J. Pratt (eds.), *The Politics of Recognising Difference. Multiculturalism Italian-Style*, 95-113. Aldershot: Ashgate.
Però, D. (2004), 'Immigrants and the Politics of Governance in Barcelona', paper presented at the 8th conference of the European Association of Social Anthropologists, Vienna, 8-12 September 2004.

Pettit, P. (1997), *Republicanism. A Theory of Freedom and Government.* Oxford: Oxford University Press.
Phillips, A. (1995), *The Politics of Presence.* Oxford: Oxford University Press.
Pitkin, H. F. (1967), *The Concept of Representation.* Berkeley: University of California Press.
Portes, A. (ed.) (2001), 'New Research and Theory on Immigrant Transnationalism', Special Issue, *Global Networks* 1 (3).
Portes, A., L. E. Guarnizo & P. Landolt (1999), 'The study of transnationalism: pitfalls and promises of an emergent research field', *Ethnic and Racial Studies* 22 (2): 217-237.
Prentoulis, N. (2001), 'On the Technology of Collective Identity: Normative Reconstructions of the Concept of EU Citizenship', *European Law Journal* 7 (2): 196-218.
Presidency Conclusions, 'Tampere European Council 1999'. www.europarl.eu.int/summits/tam_en.htm.
Preuß, U. K. (1997), 'Probleme eines Konzepts europäischer Staatsbürgerschaft', in H. Kleger (ed.), *Transnationale Staatsbürgerschaft.* Frankfurt/Main: Campus.
Preuss, U. K. (2003), 'Citizenship and the German Nation', *Citizenship Studies* 7 (1): 37-55.
Preuss, U. K., M. Everson, M. Koenig-Archibugi & E. Lefebrvre (2003), 'Traditions of Citizenship in the European Union', *Citizenship Studies* 7 (1): 3-14.
Pries, L. (ed.) (1997), *Transnationale Migration. Soziale Welt.* Sonderband 12. Baden-Baden: Nomos.
Rallu, J. L. (2004), 'Access to citizenship and integration of migrants: Lessons from the French case', paper presented at the twelfth conference of the Australian Population Association, Canberra, 15-17 September 2004. www.acsr.anu.edu.au/APA2004.
Reich, N. (2001), 'Union Citizenship – Metaphor or Source of Rights?', *European Law Journal* 7 (1): 4-23.
Rubio-Marín, R. (2000), *Immigration as a Democratic Challenge. Citizenship and Inclusion in Germany and the United States.* Cambridge: Cambridge University Press.
Rummens, J. A. (2003), 'Conceptualising Identity and Diversity: Overlaps, Intersections, and Processes', *Canadian Ethnic Studies* 35 (3): 10-25.
Saggar, S. (ed.) (1998), *Race and British Electoral Politics.* London: UCL Press.
Sassen, S. (1996), 'Losing Control?', New York: Columbia University Press.
Schibel, Y. (2004), 'Monitoring and influencing the transposition of EU immigration law. The family reunion and long term resident directives', paper presented at the European Migration Dialogue, Brussels, September 2004.
Schweizerischer Bundesrat (2001), *Botschaft zum Bürgerrecht für junge Ausländerinnen und Ausländer und zur Revision des Bürgerrechtsgesetzes.* Bern: EDMZ.
Scott, K. (2004), 'The Economics of Citizenship. Is there a Naturalization Premium?', paper presented at the conference 'Immigrant Ascension to Citizenship: Recent Policies and Economic and Social Consequences', International conference organised under the auspices of the Willy Brandt Guest Professorship's Chair International Migration and Ethnic Relations, Malmö University, 7 June 2004.
Shachar, A. (2003) 'Children of a Lesser State: Sustaining Global Inequality through Citizenship Laws', in I. M. Young & S. J. Macedo (eds.), *Child, Family, State.* NOMOS XLVI, 345-397. New York: New York University Press.
Shaw, J. (1998), 'The Interpretation of European Union Citizenship', *The Modern Law Review* 61 (3): 293-317.
Shore, C. (2004), 'Whither European Citizenship? Eros and Civilization Revisited', *European Journal of Social Theory* 1: 27-44.
Sicakkan, H. & Y. Lithman (eds.) (2004), *Envisioning Togetherness. Politics of Identity and Forms of Belonging.* New York: Edwin Mellen Press.
Simeant, J. (1997), *La cause des sans-papiers.* Paris: Presses de Science Po.

Smith, R. (2001), 'Citizenship: Political', in P. B. Baltes & N. J. Smelser (eds.), *International Encyclopedia of the Social and Behavioral Sciences*: 1857-1860.
Soininen, M. (1999), 'The "Swedish Model" as an institutional framework for immigrant membership rights', *Journal of Ethnic and Migration Studies*, 25 (4): 685-702.
Solomos, J. & L. Back (1991), 'Black political mobilisation and the struggle for equality', *The Sociological Review* 39 (2): 215-237.
Soysal, Y. (1994), *Limits of Citizenship. Migrants and Postnational Membership in Europe.* Chicago etc.: University of Chicago Press.
Spinner-Halev, J. (1994), *The Boundaries of Citizenship. Race, Ethnictiy, and Nationality in the Liberal State.* Baltimore: The Johns Hopkins University Press.
Straubhaar, T. (2003), 'Wird die Staatsangehörigkeit zu einer Klubmitgliedschaft?', in D. Thränhardt & U. Hunger (ed.), *Migration im Spannungsfeld von Globalisierung und Nationalstaat*, Leviathan Sonderheft 22, 76-89. Wiesbaden: Westdeutscher Verlag.
Strudel, S. (1996), *Votes Juifs. Itinéraires migratoires, religieux et politiques.* Paris: Presses de Sciences Po.
Thränhardt, D. (2000), 'Tainted Blood: The Ambivalence of "Ethnic" Migration in Israel, Japan, Korea, Germany and the United States', *German Policy/Politikfeldanalyse* 3. spaef.com/GPS_PUB/vın3.html.
Tiebout, C. (1956), 'A pure theory of local expenditure', *Journal of Political Economy* 64: 417-424.
Tillie, J. (1994), *Kleurrijk kiezen. Opkomst en stemgedrag van migranten tijdens de gemeenteraadsverkiezingen van 2 maart 1994.* Utrecht: Nederlands Centrum Buitenlanders.
Tillie, J. (1998), 'Explaining Migrant Voting Behaviour in the Netherlands. Combining the Electoral Research and Ethnic Studies Perspective', *Revue Européenne des Migrations Internationales* 14 (2): 71-95.
Tillie, J. (2004), 'Social Capital of Organisations and their Members: Explaining the Political Integration of Immigrants in Amsterdam', *Journal of Ethnic and Migration Studies* 30 (3): 529-541.
Tyson, A. (2001), 'The Negotiation of the European Community Directive on Racial Discrimination', *European Journal of Migration Law* 3: 111-229.
Van den Tillaart, H., M. Olde Monnikhof, S. van den Berg & J. Warmerdam (2000), *Nieuwe etnische groepen, een onderzoek onder vluchtelingen en statushouders uit Afghanistan, Ethiopië en Eritrea, Iran, Somalië en Vietnam.* Nijmegen: ITS.
Van Gunsteren, H. (1998), *A Theory of Citizenship. Organizing Plurality in Contemporary Democracies.* Boulder, Co.: Westview Press.
Van Heelsum, A. (2002), 'The relationship between political participation and civic community of migrants in the Netherlands', *Journal of International Migration and Integration* 3 (2): 179-199.
Van Heelsum, A. (2004a), *Migrantenorganisaties in Nederland, Deel 1: Aantal en soort organisaties en ontwikkelingen.* Utrecht: FORUM.
Van Heelsum, A. (2004b), *Migrantenorganisaties in Nederland, Deel 2: Het functioneren van de organisaties.* Utrecht: FORUM.
Van Heelsum, A. & J. Tillie (2000), 'Stemgedrag van migranten in de gemeenteraadsverkiezingen van 1998', in J. Tillie (ed.), *De etnische Stem, opkomst en stemgedrag van migranten tijdens de gemeenteraadsverkiezingen 1986-1998*, 18-42. Utrecht: FORUM.
Vermeersch, P. (2002), 'Ethnic mobilisation and the political conditionality of European Union accession: the case of the Roma in Slovakia', *Journal of Ethnic and Migration Studies* 28 (1): 83-101.
Vermeersch, P. (2004), 'Minority Policy in Central Europe: Exploring the Impact of the EU's Enlargement Strategy', *The Global Review of Ethnopolitics* 3 (2).

Vermeersch, P. (2003), 'EU Enlargement and Minority Rights Policies in Central Europe: Explaining Policy Shifts in the Czech Republic, Hungary and Poland', *Journal of Ethnopolitics and Minority Issues in Europe* 1.

Vertovec, S. (2000), *The Hindu Diaspora*. London: Routledge.

Waldrauch, H. (2001), *Die Integration von Einwanderern: Ein Index der rechtlichen Diskriminierung*. Frankfurt: Campus.

Waldrauch, H. & Dilek Çinar (2003), 'Staatsbürgerschaftspolitik und Einbürgerungspraxis in Österreich', in H. Fassmann & I. Stacher (eds.), *Österreichischer Migrations- und Integrationsbericht. Demographische Entwicklungen – Sozioökonomische Strukturen – Rechtliche Rahmenbedingungen*, 261-283. Klagenfurt/Celovec: Drava.

Walzer, M. (1983), *Spheres of Justice. A Defence of Pluralism and Equality*. New York: Basic Books.

Wanner, P. & G. D'Amato (2003), *Naturalisation en Suisse. Le rôle des changements législatifs sur la demande de naturalisation*. Neuchâtel: FSM.

Weil, Patrick (2001): 'Access to Citizenship. A Comparison of Twenty-Five Nationality Laws', in A. T. Aleinikoff & D. Klusmeyer (eds.), *Citizenship Today. Global Perspectives and Practices*, 17-35. Washington, DC: Carnegie Endowment for International Peace.

Weil, Patrick (2002): *Qu'est-ce qu'un Français? Histoire de la nationalité française depuis la Révolution*. Paris: Grasset.

Weiler, J. H. H. (1997), 'To be a European citizen – Eros and civilization', *Journal of European Public Policy* 4 (4): 459-519.

Weiler, J. H. H. (1999), *The Constitution of Europe: "Do the New Clothes have an Emperor?" and Other Essays on European Integration*. Cambridge: Cambridge University Press.

Wiener, A. (1997), 'Making sense of the new geography of citizenship: Fragmented citizenship in the European Union', *Theory and Society* 26: 529-560.

Young, I. M. (1990), *Justice and the Politics of Group Difference*. Princeton, NJ: Princeton University Press,

Zappala, G. & S. Castles (2000), 'Citizenship and Immigration in Australia, in A. T. Aleinikoff & D. Klusmeyer (eds.), *From Migrants to Citizens. Membership in a Changing World*, 32-81. Washington DC: Carnegie Endowment for International Peace.